Footprint Handbook

Paraguay

GEOFFREY GROESBECK

This is
Paraguay

An air of mystery hangs over this under-explored pocket of South America. From the wild impenetrable Chaco in the northwest to the lush forests of the southeast, there is an incredible diversity of flora and fauna, a number of rivers to navigate and many opportunities to experience rural tourism. Although dwarfed by its giant neighbours Brazil and Argentina, Paraguay covers some 407,000 sq km, roughly the size of California, and sits at the confluence of six important eco-regions.

This landlocked country has a strange history of intrepid missionaries, charismatic leaders and bloody wars, yet embodies a spirit of steadfastness and isolation not found elsewhere on the continent. Paraguayans are proud of their indigenous Guaraní culture, evident in the widespread use of its language, which is taught in schools and is spoken daily by roughly half of the population. Although difficult to pronounce for many outsiders, the Guaraní language does not mask the warmth of Paraguayan hospitality, perhaps best known through its ubiquitous drink yerba mate (*Ilex paraguariensis*), traditionally given to all visitors.

Today the country is part of the Latin American and Caribbean Economic System, with trade routes to Argentina and Brazil well established and an asphalt road to Bolivia finally completed. Famed for its arduous but rewarding treks, Paraguay's infamous Ruta 9, the Trans-Chaco Highway, remains one of the great road adventures in South America, and a journey along the length of either of the country's two major rivers, the Río Paraguay or the Río Paraná, is truly a once-in-a-lifetime experience.

Geoffrey Groesbeck

Best of
Paraguay

❶ Panteón Nacional de los Héroes, Asunción

At the heart of the capital, this is Paraguay's most famous and instantly recognizable building. A memorial to the country's valiant, sometimes tragic past, the pantheon is the mausoleum of the country, where the remains of Mariscal Francisco Solano López and other key figures are protected by a military guard. Page 22.

❷ Jesuit missions

The beautiful ruins of several Jesuit reducciones give an idea of the successful but short-lived religious and social project during the colonization of South America in the 17th century. The former mission settlements of Santísima Trinidad de Paraná and Jesús de Tavarangue have been recognized by UNESCO as World Heritage Sites. Page 46.

❸ Encarnación

One of Paraguay's most attractive cities, with a wide river beach and newly completed Costanera, Encarnación is best known as the country's 'Carnival Capital'. Giving Rio a run for its money, the raucous annual celebration of music and dance sees thousands of revellers lining the streets to marvel at the spectacular floats and dance the night away to the thumping samba-infused beats. Page 51.

❹ San Bernardino lakeside resort

On the eastern shore of Ypacaraí Lake, San Bernardino (known as 'San Ber') is the summer bolthole for Paraguay's rich and beautiful who come here to relax and party. The shady cobbled streets are lined with hotels, restaurants, bars and discos, while the lake is popular for water sports and pleasure cruises. Page 59.

❺ Itaipú

Paraguay's side of the second largest hydroelectric scheme in the world is a mix of titanic engineering and carefully managed environmental projects. Not without controversy, the sheer scale of the project is undeniably impressive and visitors are invited to take a panoramic tour of the power plant's spillway and dam. Page 76.

❻ The Chaco

One of the last great wilderness areas in South America, the Chaco makes up 60% of the country. From marshy palm savannah to rugged impenetrable scrub forest, it's a haven for wildlife though the area is under threat from rapid deforestation. With no urbanized areas for more than 400 km, only the isolated Mennonite communities are hardy enough to live here, and driving the Trans-Chaco Highway is not for the faint-hearted. Page 105.

Chaco savannah

Route planner

putting it all together

Paraguay is divided into two main regions separated by the Río Paraguay. **Asunción**, sits between these two areas; to the east of the river lies the **Región Oriental** (comprising approximately 40% of Paraguay's land mass) and to the west the **Región Occidental** (approximately 60%), better known simply as the Chaco. Unless coming northwest from Buenos Aires or southeast from Santa Cruz, it is best to plan your travels to either of these regions from Asunción.

The capital and eastern Paraguay

a city that means business in the fertile agricultural part of the country

Asunción, the capital and Paraguay's largest city, sits on a bay of the Río Paraguay. The continuing expansion of the city's metropolitan area means it now rubs shoulders with a dozen neighbouring cities to form Gran Asunción. This metropolis is the political and commercial heart of the country, holds some 45% of its population and has a rich history dating to 1536 (although much of its architecture dates from no earlier than the early 1800s).

The Región Oriental

Making up most of the fertile agricultural part of the country, it is its cultural and historic cradle. The towns and villages here are quiet and traditional; many have unique crafts and folklore associated with them. Paraguay's Franciscan history is well represented in this region, particularly in the towns of Altos, Caazapá and others near Lake Ypacaraí. There are also many signs of Jesuit heritage, best exemplified by the ruins of the former mission settlements at Santísima Trinidad de Paraná and Jesús de Tavarangue, declared World Heritage Sites by UNESCO in 1993, close to the city of Encarnación, now one of Paraguay's premier tourist destinations.

From Encarnación you can cross the Río Paraná to the Argentine city

Fact file

Location 25.2667° S, 57.6667° W
Capital Asunción
Time zone GMT -4 hrs; Oct-Mar GMT -3 hrs
Telephone country code +595
Currency Guaraní (PYG)

of Posadas. Roughly paralleling Paraguay's Ruta 6 for nearly 500 km, this river forms Paraguay's border with Brazil. Of the several frontier posts, the main one is the [in]famous city of Ciudad del Este, the country's second largest, and a duty-free shopper's paradise. From here you can visit Itaipú, which until recently was the largest hydroelectric dam in the world. Across the Friendship Bridge from Ciudad del Este is Foz do Iguaçu in Brazil and the magnificent Iguaçu Falls.

North of the capital
river trips and routes to Brazil and Bolivia

North of Asunción there are two main cities, the now-dangerous border town of Pedro Juan Caballero, reached from the only other northern settlement of any size, Concepción. An interesting route, if you have the time, is to travel to Concepción by river boat from the capital, passing by Mennonite communities en route. The boat ride – which must be arranged in advance from the harbour in Asunción – takes at least a day. Faster ways are via the Chaco, taking the Trans-Chaco Highway (Ruta Transchaco or Ruta 9) north and then Ruta 5 east in Pozo Colorado with some spectacular birdwatching along the way; or the more scenic option of travelling northeast across Cordillera and San Pedro departments along Ruta 3 and then west on Ruta 5 at Ybu Yaú. Beyond Concepción, the Río Paraguay leads to the Brazilian and Bolivian Pantanal, which can also be reached, weather permitting, along the poorly maintained Ruta Bahía Negra–Fuerte Olimpo road.

Western Paraguay
the wild west

The **Región Occidental**, or **Chaco**, makes up the western 60% of the country. Divided into three departments, Presidente Hayes (also known as Bajo Chaco), Boquerón and Alto Paraguay (or Alto Chaco), the Chaco begins as a marshy palm savannah, but becomes an increasingly impenetrable and dry scrub forest as it approaches the border with Bolivia. The Trans-Chaco Highway does indeed cross the Chaco to the northwest but apart from scattered military outposts (*fortines*), there are no urbanized areas for 400 km until you reach the Mennonite colonies of Filadelfia, Loma Plata and Neuland, which make up the Chaco Central region, synonymous with Boquerón Department. A relatively short distance further northwest is the former military base of Mariscal Estigarribia. After this, apart from the occasional large ranch (*estancia*) or *fortín*, there are only two tiny permanent settlements: Capitán Pablo Lagerenza to the north, and General Eugenio Garay to the northwest. This is not a region in which to venture off the beaten track alone and unprepared.

When to go

Climate

The best time to travel is August to October and the best time to see wildlife is June to July. The climate is subtropical, with a marked difference between summer and winter and often from one day to the next. December to February (summer) can be very hot and humid, with temperatures from 25°C to 40°C, and even higher in the Chaco. From June to August (winter) the temperature can range from 0°C at night to 28°C in the day. From March to May (autumn) and September to October/November (spring) the heat is less oppressive. Some rain falls each month, but the heaviest rains tend to occur from March to May. Temperatures below freezing are very rare.

Festivals

Encarnación and Villarrica vie for the best carnival celebrations (usually in February) with perhaps Encarnación just edging ahead in terms of flashiness. Villarrica's **Carnaval Guaireño** is more traditional but still spectacular. Villarrica also holds a four-day **Festival de Ñandutí** in early July, including processions and the crowning of Señorita Ñandutí. Many of Paraguay's best traditional musicians perform during the festival. Pilar hosts the **Fiesta Hawaiana** attracting tens of thousands of visitors in January and also a **fishing festival** which is said to be the largest in South America duing Holy Week. On a more modest level, there is a free (and fun) **folklore festival** every Sunday night at San Ignacio Guazú.

Weather Asunción

January	February	March	April	May	June
35°C	33°C	33°C	29°C	25°C	24°C
22°C	22°C	21°C	18°C	14°C	13°C
135mm	143mm	145mm	170mm	70mm	83mm

July	August	September	October	November	December
24°C	26°C	28°C	30°C	32°C	34°C
11°C	13°C	14°C	18°C	19°C	31°C
47mm	53mm	85mm	154mm	161mm	170mm

What to do

Adventure tourism

Paraguay is not geared up for adrenlin junkies. Being landlocked, it is not surprising that it is lacking in water sports. The lakeside resort of San Barnardino has some canoeing and waterskiing. Also on offer here are mountain biking, canopy walks and 4WD expeditions. Rappelling and zip-lining are offered at Eco Reserva Mbatoví (see page 41).

There are a few municipal toursim initiatives in the country. One of the more successful ones is at Villemi. An ambitious tour explores the Río Apa, which for some kilometres forms the border between Paraguay and Brazil.

Birdwatching

Paraguay has some spectacular birdlife with some 687 species to be spotted. Many of these are in the Chaco but the Atlantic forest is also rewarding. Getting into, and around, the protected areas is not straightforward though (see box, page 60 for further information).

Hiking

Hiking trails are limited, with the best opportunities at Eco Reserva Mbatoví close to Paraguarí on Ruta 1, Parque Nacional Ybycuí on Ruta 2 and Parque Nacionales Cerro Corá and Arroyo Yu'i-y, both in the north of the country. There are also some good trails on the Argentine side of the Iguazú Falls away from the main circuits.

History

Paraguay has an interesting history: most travellers will want to visit the Jesuit missions (brought to many people's attention by Martin Scorsese's film *The Mission*) and understand how they came to be established on the banks of the Paraná river.

The area around Pilar saw many bloody battles during the disastrous War of the Triple Alliance where over 50% of Paraguay's population were killed.

More recently the German colonies are all worth investigating, including Nueva Germani established in 1866 to create a pure Aryan colony.

Nature tourism

Tours can be arranged to even the most remote areas of the country where you are guaranteed to spot a large number of Paraguay's 171 mammals (not to mention the estimated 13,000 plant species). There are some volunteering opportunites, notably in the Atlantic forest. Don't expect it to be easy though (see box page 60, for further information).

River trips

Travelling along the Río Paraguay to Puerto Busch in the Bolivian Pantanal is truly relaxing as it is very slow! It is best done in three stages and will take around five days on the water but longer in total as you will need to wait for boats. These are working boats: the leg from Asunción to Concepción is fairly comfortable but beyond that expect very basic facilities.

Rural tourism

Staying on an estancia can be a very enoyable way to experience life in rural Paraguay. Don't expect to join in though as it is assumed that you will want to relax rather than work! For further information, see page 42.

Shopping

Paraguay has an abundance of different traditional handicrafts that make popular souvenirs and help support the local economy. See Culture, page 126, for details.

Where to stay

from ultra-luxurious hotels to estancias

Hotels

Paraguay has some of the least expensive accommodation on the continent although there are some very upmarket establishments in Asunción, Ciudad del Este and Encarnación.

Many hotels are in our $$-$ range, which are often of a good standard with private shower and toilet. However, there are very few hostels with dormitory accommodation (US$10-15 per person). Backpacker-friendly hotels are cropping up in Asunción and Encarnación, but are still relatively unknown elsewhere. Most hotels have two rates – with or without air-conditioning (the cheaper rate is often not posted so be sure to ask). Almost all rates include breakfast.

Estancias

Staying on an estancia to experience life in rural Paraguay is growing in popularity. They tend to be concentrated in the southeast and to the east and northeast of Asunción. Usually in our $$$ range, this is for full board and transportation from the main road. They often have horse riding and walking trails as well as other facilities such as tennis courts.

Price codes

Where to stay

$$$$ over US$150

$$$ US$66-150

$$ US$30-65

$ under US$30

Price of a double room in high season, including taxes.

Restaurants

$$$ over US$12

$$ US$7-12

$ US$6 and under

Prices for a two-course meal for one person, excluding drinks or service charge.

Food & drink

A typical local food is *chipa*, a cheese bread that comes in a number of varieties: *almidón*, made with yuca flour; *barrero*, made with corn flour; *manduví*, made with peanuts (better warm than cold). *Chipa so'o* is maize bread with minced meat filling; *chipa guazú* is made with fresh corn; *sopa paraguaya* is a kind of sponge of ground maize and cheese. These make a great side dish, or can be enjoyed on their own. *Soyo* is a soup of different meats and vegetables; *albóndiga* a soup of meat balls; *bori bori* another type of soup with diced meat, vegetables, and small balls of maize mixed with cheese. The beef is excellent in the better restaurants (best cuts are *lomo* and *lomito*) and can be enjoyed with *chorizo, morcilla, chipa guazú, sopa paraguaya* and a variety of salads. *Parrillada completa* is recommended and there are many *churrascarías* (barbecues) serving huge quantities of meat, with salad, vegetables and pasta. River fish include *surubí* and *dorado*, which are prepared in many different ways. Although vegetarian restaurants are scarce, there are lots of fruits, salads and vegetables, as well as the non-meat varieties of *empanada*, such as *choclo, palmito* or *cuatro quesos*.

> **Tip...**
>
> Lunch is usually served 1130-1300 in most restaurants and bars. Evening meals are hard to find in small towns, but options exist in larger cities.

Drink

The most popular national drink is *tereré* (cold yerba mate with digestive herbs) for warm days and hot yerba mate to warm you up on cold days (see box page 52). *Cocido* is a type of tea made by burning (traditionally with a red ember) the yerba with some sugar; this can be served with or without milk. Paraguayan ales are very good, the better brands being Kure Dumas, Korok and Astoria. These are golden ales and porters, but you can find traditional lagers and pilsner beers as well. The better brands of the national sugar cane-based spirit, *caña*, include Aristocrata (known as 'Ari'), Fortín and Tres Leones. You can find most global brand soft drinks, including Guaraná (from Brazil). *Mosto* is a very sweet but refreshing juice made from sugar cane.

Essential Asunción

Finding your feet

Silvio Pettirossi International Airport is in Luque, 16 km northeast of the city centre, from which taxis, buses and an airport-to-hotel minibus service run. It takes about 45 minutes to get from the airport to town. The bus terminal, Terminal de Omnibus Asunción, T021-551740, www.mca.gov.py/toa.htm, is south of the centre at the intersection of Avenidas Fernando de la Mora y República Argentina, 30-45 minutes away by taxi or bus. See also Transport, page 35.

Best places to stay

Amalfi, page 28
Las Margaritas, page 28
Black Cat Hostel, page 29
Zaphir, page 29

Getting around

Most of the sights are in a relatively small area by the river, which can easily be covered on foot. Likewise, many central hotels and restaurants are within walking distance of this area. Places outside the city's centre, for example Villa Morra, are easily reached by taxi (preferable) or bus (for those with time to spare).

There is an extensive public bus network covering the city. Buses stop at signs before every street corner and supposedly run every eight minutes 0600-2400, though this is only true on the more popular routes and many stop at 2200. The destination

Tip...

If going by taxi, give the driver the specific street address but also the name of the nearest intersection. The often-used 'casi' (near) and 'esquina' (corner) both mean 'at the corner of'. Almost all locations in Asunción are referred to in this manner.

will usually be posted in the front window. Asunción is very spread out and transport is slow; you need to allow 60-90 minutes to get beyond the city limits. Taxis are plentiful and can be hailed on the street or found at a taxi rank.

When to go

Asunción is warm and humid throughout the year but the winter (May to September) is cooler and more pleasant with less rain. Summer can be uncomfortably hot. See weather chart on page 11.

Best restaurants

Fabio Rolandi's, page 30
Lido Bar, page 31
Mburicao, page 30
El Molino, page 31
San Roque, page 31
Tapei, page 31

Time required

A couple of days are enough to get to know the city centre and visit the major sights.

Asunción

Asunción (population 515,587) was founded in 1536 on the eastern bank of a calm bay in the Río Paraguay. It is the longest continually inhabited area in the River Plate Basin and in colonial times was referred to as the 'Mother of Cities' because it was from here that both missionaries and military expeditions set off to establish other cities. The centre is a testament to 19th-century ideals, with names reflecting its heroes and battles. Tree-lined avenues, parks and squares break up the rigid grid system. In July and August the city is drenched in colour from the prolific pink bloom of lapacho trees, which grow everywhere.

Best for
Culture ▪ History ▪ Walking tours

grand colonial buildings, shady plazas and the capital's key sights

Asunción is often called 'La Capital Tranquila' (the peaceful capital), and is indeed a tranquil city in spite of its relentless pace of growth and commercialization. Asunción's historic centre (along with a few other areas throughout the city) has recently undergone something of a renaissance in terms of visitor popularity and government support, and a number of tours now take in its best-known buildings and sights. However, the restoration of several significant buildings (such as Palacio de Gobierno) – initially timed to coincide with Paraguay's independence bicentennial in 2011 – still continues. As a result, hours of operation for these locations may change without advance notice.

Asunción

Where to stay 🛏
1 Amalfi *C4*
3 Aspen Apart Hotel *C1*
4 Asunción Palace *B1*
5 Bavaria *A6*
6 Black Cat Hostel *A3*
8 Cecilia *B6*
9 Chaco *B4*
10 City *C3*

11 Crowne Plaza *B6*
13 El Viajero Hostel *C3*
14 Granados Park *B2*
15 La Casita de la Abuela
    Hostal Verde *C1*
16 La Española *C4*
17 Las Margaritas *B2*
18 Maison Suisse *A6*
19 Palmas del Sol *A6*

20 Paramanta *A6*
21 Portal del Sol *A6*
23 Sabe Center *B4*
24 Sheraton *A6*
25 Westfalenhaus *A6*
26 Zaphir *B1*

Restaurants 🍴
1 Bar Leo *B1*

La Recova to Palacio de Gobierno

At the bottom of Avenida Colón, just before it joins El Paraguayo Independiente, are the colonial façades of **La Recova**: a line of shops selling local arts and crafts. This area should not be overlooked by those seeking bargains. The main river port and **Aduanas y Puertos** (Customs) are at this same junction. Every Saturday afternoon from 1500 there are cultural activities at the port (**Puerto Abierto**). Continue along El Paraguayo Independiente to a small plaza on your left with a statue of the former dictator, Alfredo Stroessner. After his deposition, the statue was crushed and placed inside a block of concrete, only his hands and face protruding. Next to this is the **Palacio de Gobierno** (1857), currently undergoing restoration, built in the style of Versailles by Alan Taylor as a palace for President Francisco Solano López (1860-1669). Taylor used child labour to finish the project as all the adult men were enlisted to fight in the Triple Alliance War. It now houses government departments. Down the side of the palace towards the river is a platform for viewing the back of the building.

Directly opposite the palace is the **Manzana de la Rivera** ⓘ *Ayolas 129 y El Paraguayo Independiente, T021-445085, Mon-Sat 0700-2000, museum and cultural centre Mon-Fri 0900-2100, Sat 1000-2000, Sun 1000-1900, library Mon-Fri 0700-1900, Sat 0800-1200*, a patio area and 10 buildings, nine of which are restored, dating from the 1700s. These include: **Casa Viola**, with **Museo Memoria de la Ciudad** and its historical photos and city information; **Casa Clari**, with exhibition halls and a bar; the **Miguel Acevedo cultural centre**; the **Ruy Díaz de Guzmán auditorium**; and **Casa Vertúa**, the municipal library. These collectively represent the most complete set of colonial-era buildings in the city. If pressed for time, set aside a few minutes for the Museo Memoria in Casa Viola at least, which in addition to tracing the city's history has poignant exhibits on Paraguayans who suffered under the Stroessner dictatorship.

2 Bellini *B2*
3 Bolsi *B3*
4 Café Literario *B4*
5 El Bar de la Preferida *B6*
6 El Molino *A6*
7 La Flor de la Canela *A5*
8 La Vienesa *B3*
11 Lido Bar *B3*
12 Munich *A4*

13 Paseo Carmelitas *A6*
14 San Roque *B5*
15 Taberna Española *C1*

Bars & clubs 🎵
16 Britannia Pub *B5*
17 Rivera *B2*

East to the cathedral

A block away from the palace is the **Congreso Nacional**, built in steel and glass representing a huge ship moored on the river bank and incorporating part of the old Congress building. On **Plaza de la Independencia** there is a small memorial to those who died in the struggle for democracy (also look out for statues of the frog and the dog). On the plaza are: the **Antiguo Colegio Militar** (1588) originally a Jesuit College, now home to government ministries; the **Cabildo** (1844-1854) ① *T021-443094, http://cabildoccr.gov.py, Mon-Fri 0900-1900, Sat 0800-1200, free*, since 2003 the **Centro Cultural de la República** ① *T021-443094, http://cabildoccr.gov.py,* with temporary exhibitions, indigenous and religious art, museum of music, film and video on the top floor; and the **Catedral Metropolitana** ① *T021-449512, not always open, but hours posted in front, it's possible to view the interior before, after or during Mass, usually around 1100 daily,* dating to the mid-17th century (rebuilt 1842-1849). The cathedral's altar, decorated with Jesuit and Franciscan silver, is very beautiful.

Tip...

Don't be confused: Plaza de la Independencia is often referred to as Plaza Constitución or Plaza Juan de Salazar.

South of Plaza de la Independencia

From Plaza de la Independencia turn right onto Alberdi and to your right is the **Correos** (old post office), formerly the Palacio Patri, with a courtyard and a small museum (the building is reportedly being restored). At Alberdi and Presidente Franco is the **Teatro Municipal Ignacio Pane** ① *T021-445169, www. teatromunicipal.com.py for information on events*, fully restored to its former belle époque glory.

★Plaza de los Héroes

Mariscal Estigarribia becomes Palma at its intersection with Independencia Nacional (the names of all streets running east to west change at this point). On Plaza de los Héroes is the **Panteón Nacional de los Héroes** ① *Palma y Chile, daily, hours not posted*, which is based on Les Invalides in Paris, begun during the Triple Alliance War and finished in 1937. It contains the tombs of the presidents Carlos Antonio López and his son Francisco Solano López; Mariscal José Félix Estigarribia, the victor of the Chaco War; an unknown child-soldier; and other national heroes. The child-soldiers honoured in the Panteón were boys aged 12-16 who fought at the Battle of Acosta Ñu in the War of the Triple Alliance, 15 August 1869. Most of the boys died and somewhere between 60-70% of adult Paraguayan men were killed during the war. Plaza de los Héroes is one of four separate but contiguous squares with different names (the others being Plaza de la Libertad, Plaza Juan E O'Leary and Plaza de la Democracia) but these are very rarely used; the entire area is sometimes referred to as **Plaza de la Democracia**.

West of Plaza de los Héroes

On weekdays in the Plaza Libertad (at Chile y Oliva) there are **covered market stalls** selling traditional Paraguayan arts and crafts in wood, cotton and leather. Along Palma indigenous women sell colourful woven bags, beads and baskets. You may be approached by indigenous men selling bags, whistles, bows and arrows or feather headdresses.

A few blocks further along Palma near its intersection with Alberdi is the Senatur office (see **Tourist information**, page 27), which has craft stalls for those not wishing to buy on the street. On Saturday morning, until 1200, Palma becomes a pedestrian area, with stalls selling arts, crafts and clothes, and during the summer there is entertainment outside the tourist office. On Sunday there are stalls selling second-hand and antique items around Plaza de los Héroes and in front of the Nueva América department store on Independencia Nacional. If looking for more handicraft and traditional items, also visit the nearby Plaza de la Democracia bordering Oliva y NS de la Asunción. But note that certain crafts, such as the famous *ñandutí* ('spiderweb' lace), should be purchased directly from its makers in the nearby town of Itaguá.

From Palma turn right at 14 de Mayo to visit the **Casa de la Independencia** (1772) ⓘ *14 de Mayo y Pdte Franco, T021-493918, www.casadelaindependencia.org. py, Mon-Fri 0800-1800, Sat 0800-1300, free, has toilets*, with a historical collection; the 1811 anti-colonial revolution was plotted here.

South of Plaza de los Héroes

The **Iglesia de Encarnación** ⓘ *14 de Mayo y Víctor Haedo, T021-490860*, was partially restored after a fire in 1889 by an Italian immigrant who offered his services gratis on condition that he be free to select the best materials. Thanks to a 2013 publicity campaign, the Ministry of Public Works has committed to a complete restoration of the church. In spite of the ongoing work, it is a tranquil place to end your tour.

Barrio San Jerónimo

Asunción's colourful barrio turístico

Paraguay is experimenting with a number of newly designated tourist destinations in Asunción, San Bernardino, Villarrica and Encarnación.

In Asunción, the best known is Barrio San Jerónimo which is undergoing a complete makeover yet retains much of its original character. The neighbourhood, which is still primarily residential, dates from the 19th century and retains many interesting historic buildings. Located at the far edge of the centre and southwest of the Costanera, the atmosphere here is decidedly eclectic, with brightly painted, flower-bedecked houses (many of which have belonged to the same families for generations) and narrow cobbled alleyways. There is an ambitious plan to build restaurants, cafés and bars along Piraveve and elsewhere in the area to establish it as a cultural centre, along the lines of Bueno Aires' La Boca neighbourhood.

East of Plaza de Héroes

The **Estación Central del Ferrocarril Carlos Antonio López Eligio** ⓘ *Ayala y México, just below Plaza Uruguaya, T021-447848,* was built 1861-1864 with British and European help. Paraguay had the first passenger carrying railway in South America. No trains now run from the station, but it has a small **museum** ⓘ *Mon-Fri 0800-1600, US$2.35,* featuring the old ticket office, machinery from Wolverhampton and Battersea and the first steam engine in Paraguay, the *Sapucaí* (1861). **Plaza Uruguaya**, at the nexus of México, Eligio Ayala, 25 de Mayo and Antequera, with its shady trees and fountain is another spot to stop and rest in the daytime. From here take Mariscal Estigarribia towards Plaza de los Héroes.

Museo Nacional de Bellas Artes and around

Heading out of the centre along Avenida Mariscal López, the **Museo Nacional de Bellas Artes** ⓘ *E Ayala 1345 y Curupayty, T021-211578, www.cultura.gov.py, Tue-Fri 0700-1800, Sat 0800-1400, free, guided tour,* shows the development of Paraguayan art and its European precursors, largely the collection of Juan Silvano Godoy.

The **Museo Histórico Militar** ⓘ *in the Ministry of National Defence, Mcal López y 22 de Septiembre, T021-223965, Mon-Fri 0700-1300, free; surrender passport on entry,* has articles from both the Triple Alliance and the Chaco wars. These include blood-stained flags from the Triple Alliance as well as clothes and personal possessions of Francisco Solano López and his Irish mistress, Eliza Lynch.

The national cemetery, **Cementerio Recoleta** ⓘ *Av Mcal López y Chóferes del Chaco,* is not to be missed. It resembles a miniature city with tombs in various architectural styles. It contains the tomb of Madame Lynch (ask a guide to show you the location) and, separately, the tomb of her baby daughter Corrine (Entrada 3 opposite Gran Unión supermarket) as well as many mausoleums of the country's most important families.

Beyond Chóferes del Chaco, between Avenida Mcal López and Avenida España, is **Villa Morra**, a smart residential and commercial zone with bars, restaurants and shopping centres.

Along Avenida España

Museo Etnográfico Dr Andrés Barbero ⓘ *España 217 y Mompox, T021-441696, www.museobarbero.org.py, Tue-Fri 0700-1100, 1500-1700, free,* houses a good collection of tools and weapons of the various Guaraní cultures. The **Centro de Artes Visuales** ⓘ *Grabadores del Cabichuí (entre Cañada y Emeterio Miranda, T021-607996, exhibitions open Thu-Sat 1530-2000, shop and café Wed-Sat 1530-2000,* includes contemporary art in the **Museo del Barro** ⓘ *T021-607996, www. museodelbarro.org, Tue 1530-2000, Wed-Sat 0900-1200 and 1530-2000, free, guided tours US$3.25,* the most popular museum in the country (the museum shop sells reproductions of ceramic figurines and other works), and the highly recommended **Museo de Arte Indígena** ⓘ *www.museodelbarro.org/exhibicion/museo-de-arte-*

indigena, which contains indigenous art and outstanding displays of rarely seen colonial art. To get there take bus 30 or 44A from the centre past Shopping del Sol, ask driver for Cañada.

Jardín Botánico y Zoológico

Six kilometres east, the 245-ha **Jardín Botánico y Zoológico** ⓘ *Av Artigas y Primer Presidente, T021-663311, www.mca.gov.py/zoo.htm, daily 0700-1700, US$1*, lies along the Río Paraguay, on the former estate of the López family. The gardens are not as exuberant as they might be, given the location, but they are pleasant and well maintained, with signed walks and a rose garden, and are bordered by the 18-hole Asunción Golf Club. In addition to a zoo claiming almost 340 species of flora and fauna, this is a good place to buy local crafts including jewellery and cloth bags, but you'll want insect repellent if taking any of the side trails.

In the gardens are the former residence of Carlos Antonio López, a two-storey typical Paraguayan country house with verandas, now housing a **Museo de Historia Natural** and a library, and that of his ill-starred son Francisco Solano López, a two-storey European-inspired mansion which is now the **Museo de Historia Natural e Indigenista y Herbario** ⓘ *Mon-Sat 0730-1130, 1300-1730, Sun 0900-1300*. Both museums are free although neither is in good condition. To get there take bus No 2, 6, 23 or 40, US$0.60, 35 minutes from Luis A Herrera, or No24, 35 or 44B from Oliva or Cerro Corá; taxis are permitted past the entrance and can pick up/drop off in front of the zoo and museums.

Riverfront

Asunción's riverfront – once a ramshackle collection of dilapidated shacks and unfinished projects – has recently undergone something of a transformation, and is now promoted as a tourist destination in itself. The riverfront area runs from the Puerto Fénix complex in the San Blas neighbourhood in the north to the ferry terminal (for crossing to the Argentine side) at the end of Florentino Oviedo in the south, but most of the action and sights are found along Avenida Costanera which hugs the inside of the bay. The makeover is ongoing: Puerto Abierto has weekly cultural activities, small cafés are starting to appear, and one can rent bikes and loll about on the strand. All river trips along the Río Paraguay start from here as well.

Around Asunción

day trips from the city taking in villages and countryside

Luque

East of Asunción Luque (population 361,662; take bus No 30), technically a city in its own right but essentially a part of Asunción, was awarded to the conquistador Miguel Antón de Luque in 1635 and settled by Franciscan missionaries soon after. It has an attractive central plaza with some well-preserved colonial buildings and a pedestrianized area with outdoor cafés. A lovely 25-ha park, **Ñu Guasú**, is located close to the airport and makes an excellent spot to relax and observe the various events, from bicycle racing to sky-diving. The park also has walking and jogging paths, exercise stations, a food court, football pitches, and – much rarer in Paraguay – tennis and basketball courts. Entrance is free and the park is policed. Luque is famous for the making of Paraguayan harps and guitars and for fine filigree jewellery in silver and gold, which is available to buy at very good prices from shops on the main street. It also is aware of its colonial heritage: the partial demolition in 2012 of two colonial-era houses in its centre was halted by the government. **Tourist information** is available at Plaza General Aquino, where there's a mausoleum of José Elizardo Aquino, a hero of the disastrous War of the Triple Alliance.

There are some fine musical instrument shops on the road to Luque along Avenida Aviadores del Chaco, including **Guitarras Sanabria** ⓘ *Av Aviadores del Chaco 2574 y San Blas, T021-614974, www.arpasgsanabria.com.py*, one of the best-known firms. For online information on Luque, see www.luque.gov.py.

San Lorenzo

On the southeast outskirts of Asunción, at Km 12, is the fast-growing city of San Lorenzo (population 320,878), now the fourth largest in Paraguay, founded in 1775. To get there, follow Ruta 2 (Mariscal Estigarribia Highway) or take bus Nos 12, 18, 56 or 26 and get off at the central plaza. There is a daily market in front of the astonishingly beautiful pale blue, neo-Gothic cathedral, unique in style for Paraguay and justly declared a Monumento Artístico Cultural e Histórico by the government, after some 50 years in the making (1919-1968). The **Museo Antropológico, Arqueológico y Etnográfico Guido Boggiani** ⓘ *Bogado 888 y Saturio Ríos, 1½ blocks from plaza, T021-584717, www.portalguarani.com (under 'Museums and cultural centres'), or see Facebook, Tue-Fri 1500-1800, Sat 0900-1200 and 1500-1800; ring the bell if door is shut*, is staffed by a very helpful lady who explains the exhibits, which include rare Chamacoco feather art, and a well-displayed collection of tribal items from the Guaraní and Zamuco of the northern Chaco from the turn of the 20th century. There is a wonderful gift shop with items from more than 40 different indigenous communities. The shop across the road also sells crafts at good prices. Three blocks north is the **Universidad Nacional de Asunción**, the country's oldest and largest university.

Day trips from Asunción

Many villages close to Asunción can be visited on a day trip: for example **Areguá** and **San Bernardino** on Lago Ypacaraí (see page 59); **Altos** (see page 59), with great views over the lake; and **Itauguá** (see page 58), the centre for traditional *ñandutí* 'spider web' lace and handicrafts.

Alternatively take a tour with any travel agent (see What to do, page 35) for the Circuito de Oro or the Camino Franciscano. Destinations for both tours vary from operator to operator, but nearly all leave from the lower level of the bus station.

Circuito de Oro Tours of the Circuito de Oro tend to include (by distance from Asunción), Fernando de la Mora, San Lorenzo, Juan Augusto Saldívar, Itá, Yaguarón,

Paraguarí, Piribebuy, Caacupé, Ypacaraí, Itauguá and Capiatá. The circuit covers 160 km on paved roads on Rutas 1 and 2 and takes seven to eight hours, best done over two days. The route goes through the rolling hills of the Cordillera, no more than 650 m high, which are beautiful, with hidden waterfalls and a number of spas: Chololó, Pirareté (near Piribebuy) and Pinamar (between Piribebuy and Paraguarí) are the most developed.

Camino Franciscano The Camino Franciscano is similar but longer, and some towns from the Circuito de Oro overlap; it usually includes some combination of the historical towns of Capiatá, Ypané, Itá, Yaguarón, Villarrica, Valenzuela, Piribebuy, Caacupé, Caazapá, San Juan Neopomuceno, Tobatí, Atyrá and Altos, using Rutas 1 and 8 and several smaller roads.

Listings Asunción *map p20*

Tourist information

Secretaría Nacional de Turismo
Palma 468, T021-494110/441530,
www.senatur.gov.py or
www.paraguay.travel. Daily 0700-1900.
Staff have information on all parts of Paraguay, free map available; also has a bookstore. Both the airport and bus terminal have tourist information desks. Check for special tours being run from the tourist office, sometimes run by Senatur, sometimes in conjunction with agencies. The city of Asunción's municipal website **www.mca.gov. py** also has up-to-date information in Spanish (see also Facebook: asuncionmuni), as does the Cabildo (see page 139) which intermittently publishes an official bulletin of cultural news and events.

Where to stay

Hotel bills do not usually include service charge. Look out for special offers.

For Asunción's **Sheraton ($$$$)** see www.sheraton-asuncion.com.py; or **Crowne Plaza ($$$$)** see www. crowneasuncion.com.py. Near the bus terminal, there are several hotels on Av F de la Mora and quieter places on C Cedro, adjoining Mora, all quite similar; turn left from front of terminal, 2 mins' walk.

$$$$-$$$ Granados Park
Estrella y 15 de Agosto, T021-497921,
www.granadospark.com.py.
Luxury, top-quality hotel, range of suites with all facilities, good restaurant **Il Mondo**.

$$$$-$$$ Hotel Westfalenhaus
Sgto 1° M Benítez 1577 entre Kuarajhy y Prof Fernández, Barrio Miraflores de Trinidad, T021-280532, www. westfalenhaus.com.py.
Comfortable, German-run, half board, weekly rates and self-catering apartments, pool, safe deposit box,

international restaurant, **Piroschka**, gym, massage and spa, English, German and Spanish spoken.

$$$$-$$$ Resort Yacht y Golf Club Paraguayo
14 km from town, at Lambaré, on own beach on the Río Paraguay, T021-906121, www.resortyacht.com.py.
7 restaurants and cafés, super luxury, with pool, gym, spa, golf, tennis, airport transfers; many extras free, special deals.

$$$$-$$$ Sabe Center
25 de Mayo y México, T021-450093, www.sabecenterhotel.com.py.
Luxury hotel in modern tower, with all facilities, discounts available. English and Spanish spoken.

$$$ Aspen Apart Hotel
Ayolas 581 y Gral Díaz, T021-496066, www.aspen.com.py.
Modern, lots of marble, 50 suites and apartments, pool, sauna, gym, cheaper longer stays.

$$$ Cecilia
Estados Unidos 341 y Estigarribia, T021-210365, www.hotelcecilia.com.py.
Comfortable suites, weekend specials, pool with a view, sauna, gym, airport transfers, parking, medical service.

$$$ Chaco
Caballero 285 y Estigarribia, T021-492066, www.hotelchaco.com.py.
Central 1970s hotel, parking nearby, rooftop swimming pool, bar, good restaurant ($$$).

$$$ Las Margaritas
Estrella y 15 de Agosto, T021-448765, www.lasmargaritas.com.py.
Modern, central business hotel, safe in room, restaurant, terrace grill, gym, sauna, pool. English, German, Portuguese spoken. Recommended.

$$$ Maison Suisse
Malutín 482, Villa Morra, T021-600003, www.maisonsuisse.info.
Convenient for shops, restaurants and bars, rooms with disabled access, pool, garden, gym, buffet breakfast in 'Suizoguayo' style. Also has **Casa Suiza**, Senador Long 389, T021-603492.

$$$-$$ Paramanta
Av Aviadores del Chaco 3198, T021-607053, www.paramantahotel.com.py.
Midway between airport and centre, buses stop outside, bar, restaurant, pool, gym, gardens, and many other services. English, German, Portuguese spoken.

$$ Amalfi
Caballero 877 y Fulgencio R Moreno y Manuel Domínguez, T021-441162, www.hotelamalfi.com.py.
Modern, comfortable, spacious rooms, frigobar, safe downstairs, small bar and *comedor*. Recommended.

$$ Asunción Palace
Colón 415 y Estrella, T021-492151, www.asuncionhotelpalace.com.
Historic building dating from 1858. 24 rooms, fridge, very helpful, elegant, laundry. English spoken.

$$ Bavaria
Chóferes del Chaco 1010, T021-600966, www.hotel-bavaria-py.com.
Comfortable, colonial style, beautiful garden, pool, good value rooms and suites with kitchens, fridge, English, German spoken, very helpful staff.

$$ City
NS de la Asunción con Humaitá, T021-491497, www.cityhotel.com.py.
Good, all meals available in restaurant.

$$ La Española
Herrera 142 y F Yegros, T021-449280, www.hotellaespanola.galeon.com.

Central, poor breakfast, credit cards accepted, airport pick-up, laundry, luggage storage, restaurant, parking.

$$ Palmas del Sol
España 202, T021-449485, www.hotelportaldelsol.com.
Linked to **Portal del Sol**, very helpful, good buffet-style breakfast, a/c and fan, small pool, English, German spoken.

$$ Portal del Sol
Av Denis Roa 1455 y Santa Teresa, T021-609395, www.hotelportaldelsol.com.
Comfortable hotel, some rooms sleep 4, free airport pick-up, pool.

$$ Zaphir
Estrella 955 y Colón, T490258, zaphir@pla.net.py.
Ideal location. Rather dingy looking but cosy, clean, and quiet, Wi-Fi accessible in rooms. Very friendly staff. Highly recommended.

$ Black Cat Hostel
Eligio Ayala 129 casi Independencia Nacional, T021-449827, www.hostelblackcat.com.
Central backpacker hostel in a historic building, dorms for 8 and 16, private rooms for 1-2 ($$), shared bath, helpful with travel advice, breakfast included, English spoken. Recommended.

$ El Viajero Asunción
Alberdi 734, T021-444563, www.elviajerohostels.com/fr/hostel-asuncion.
Private and shared dorms all en suite

with a/c. Breakfast included. Cable TV and DVDs. Wide common areas, swimming pool.

$ La Casita de la Abuela Hostal Verde
Hernandarias 1074 entre Jejui y Manduvira, T981-468090, karai_pyhare@hotmail.com.
New but already hugely popular with backpackers and NGO workers. Centrally located. Rooms for 4-8. Wi-Fi, cable TV, A/c, kitchen, enclosed parking lot. Owner Javier speaks English and French and is very helpful.

Out of the city: San Lorenzo

$$$ Estancia Oñondivemi
Tourism farm, Km 27.5 on Ruta 1 just past the turn off to Ruta 2, Juan Augusto Saldivar, 30 mins from Asunción, T029-5 20344 or T981-441460, onondivemi@ onondivemi.com.py.
A pleasant escape from the city. Serves all meals, food organically grown on site. Horse riding, fishing, swimming, nature walks (they have a nearby property with a waterfall, lovely for swimming), attractive accommodation with a/c, cheaper with fan. Groups welcome.

Camping
If camping, take plenty of insect repellent. Pleasant site at the **Jardín Botánico**, tents and vehicles permitted, cold showers and 220v electricity, busy at weekends. Lock everything in vehicle.

Restaurants

Many restaurants are outside the scope of the map. A few restaurants close at weekends, but may open at night. A good meal in the food halls at the shopping malls, which you pay for by weight, as you do in some of the city centre restaurants, is about US$2.30-4. Average price of a good meal in quality restaurants: US$20-25. The following are open most days of the week, day and night. For Spanish-language reviews see www.asunciongourmet.blogspot.com.

$$$ Acuarela
Mcal López casi San Martín, T021-601750, www.acuarela.com.py.
Very good *churrascaría* and other Brazilian dishes.

$$$ Bolsi
Estrella 399 y Alberdi, T021-491841, www.bolsi.com.py.
One of Asunción's longest-operating eateries. Enormously popular. Wide choice of wines, good for breakfast, excellent food (Sun 1200-1430) in large servings. Has great diner next door, lower prices, also popular.

$$$ Ciervo Blanco
José A Flores 3870 casi Radiooperadores del Chaco, T021-212918, ciervoblanco@yahoo.com.
For meat dishes and *parrillada* and Paraguayan music shows.

$$$ Fabio Rolandi's
Mcal López y Infante Rivarola, T021-610447, www.restauranterolandi.com.
Delicious pasta, steak and fish. Recommended.

$$$ La Pérgola Jardín
Perú 240 y José Bergés, T021-214014, www.lapergola.com.py.

Under the same ownership as **Bolsi**, excellent.

$$$ Mburicao
González Rioobó 737 y Chaco Real, T021-660048, www.mburicao.com.
Mediterranean food. Highly recommended.

$$$ Paulista Grill
San Martín casi Mcal López, T021-608624, www.paulistagrill.com.py.
A good *churrascaría*, good value, cheaper in the week, popular with groups.

$$$ Shangrila
Aviadores del Chaco y San Martín, T021-661618, www.shangri-la.com.py.
Very good food at upmarket Chinese.

$$$ Sukiyaki
Hotel Uchiyamada, Constitución 763 y Luis A de Herrera, T021-222038.
Good Japanese.

$$$ Taberna Española
Ayolas 631 y General Díaz, T021-441743.
Spanish food, very good.

$$$-$$ El Chef Peruano
General Garay 431 y Del Maestro, T021-605756.
Good-quality Peruvian food, popular with groups.

$$$-$$ Tierra Colorada Gastro
Santísima Trinidad 784 y Tte Fernández, T021-663335, http://tierracoloradagastro.com.
Out of the centre in Barrio Mburucuya, toward Parque Ñu Guasu in Luque. Paraguayan-fusion dishes, deliberately healthy, many using indigenous recipes and produce from farms in the area; good reputation.

$$ Bellini
Palma 459 y 14 de Mayo.

3-course pasta buffet or à la carte, good value and popular.

$$ Lido Bar
Plaza de los Héroes, Palma y Chile, T021-446171. Daily 0700-2300.
An institution in Asunción, great location across from Panteón, loads of character. Good for breakfast, empanadas and watching the world go by. Good quality and variety, famous for fish soup, delicious, very popular. Recommended.

$$ Munich
Eligio Ayala 163, T021-447604.
Pleasant, old-fashioned, with a shady patio, popular with business people.

$$ San Roque
Eligio Ayala y Tacuary, T021-446015.
Traditional, 'an institution' and one of the oldest restaurants in town, relatively inexpensive. Recommended.

$ La Vienesa
Alberdi y Oliva, T021-612793, www.lavienesa.com.py.
Wide menu, meat dishes, fish, pasta, pizza, Mexican, lots of breads and sweets, coffee. Also does by weight and take away. Popular at lunchtime. Also at Av España y Dominicana, Villa Morra.

$ Tapei
Tte Fariña 1049 y Brasil y Estados Unidos, T021-201756.
Serves stylish Chinese and vegetarian by weight. Recommended.

Cafés and snacks

Bar Leo
Colón 462 y Olivia, T021-490333.
Small, clean place for lunch buffet, takeaway and empanadas and tortas.

Café Literario
Estigarribia 456, T021-491640. Mon-Fri 1600-2200.
Cosy café/bar, books and good atmosphere. Occasional cultural events with Alianza Francesa.

El Bar de la Preferida
Estados Unidos 341 y 25 de Mayo, T021-202222, www.hotelcecilia.com.py/ index-3.html.
Bar with meals served by kilo, Mon-Sat from 1200, different availability each day. Part of **Hotel Cecilia** and not to be confused with restaurant by the same name.

El Café de Acá
Tte Vera 390 casi Dr Mora, T021-623983, www. elcafedeaca.com. Serving coffee as in the old days.

> **Tip...**
> Most cheap lunch places close around 1600.

El Molino
España 382 y Brasil, T021-225351.
Good value, downstairs for sandwiches and home-made pastries, upstairs for full meals in a nice setting, good service and food (particularly steaks) but pricey. Bakery as well. Recommended.

Heladería París
6 locations: Brasilia y Abelardo Brugada, Roca Argentina 982, Quesada y San Roque González, Felix Bogado y 18 Julio, Julio Correa y Molas López 143, and NS de Asunción y Quinta Avenida, www.hparis.com.py.
Café/bar/ice cream parlour. Popular.

La Flor de la Canela
Tacuary 167 y Eligio Ayala, T021-498928, www.laflordelacanela.com.py.
Cheap Peruvian lunches.

Michael Bock
Pres Franco 828, T021-495847.
Excellent bread and sweet shop, specializing in German pastries.

Quattro D (4D)
San Martín y Dr Andrade, T021-615168.
Ice cream parlour offering great range of flavours, also weekday lunches from about US$1 and up.

Bars and clubs

Bars
The best up-to-date online source for bars and clubs in Asunción, Ciudad del Este and anywhere else in Paraguay is www.asunfarra.com.py. *Asunción Viva* is a weekly listing of what's going on in the city; its monthly version costs US$1.65 (free at tourist office).

Paseo Carmelitas, Av España y Malutín, Villa Morra, small but upscale mall has several popular bars, such as **El Bar**, **Kamastro**, **Kilkenney Irish Pub**, **Liquid** and the very chic **Sky Resto & Lounge** (T021-600940, www.skylounge.com. py) as well as restaurants and shops. To get there, take bus 30 from Oliva, which goes along Mcal López, but returns on España, or bus 31 to Mcal López.

Britannia Pub
Cerro Corá 851, T021-443990, www.britannia-pub.com. Evenings only, closed Mon.
Good variety of drinks, German spoken, popular expat hangout, book exchange.

Café Bohemia
Senador Long 848 casi España, T021-662191.
Original decor and atmosphere, Mon and Tue live blues/jazz, alternative at weekends.

Déjà Vu
Galería Colonial, Av España casi San Rafael, T021-615098.
Popular, open every day from 0800.

Rivera
Estrella con 14 de Mayo y Alberdi.
Central bar on 2nd floor, balcony, good for drinks and music.

Clubs
Av Brasilia has a collection of clubs such as **Ristretto Café & Bar** (No 671 y Siria, T021-224614, http://ristrettocafebar. jimdo.com) and **Mouse Cantina** (No 803 y Patria, T021-228794).

Café Proa
Padre Juan Pucheú 549 casi España at same corner as French Embassy, T021-222456.
Tango classes every night, light snacks and drinks, very pleasant.

Coyote
Sucre 1655 casi San Martín, T021-662114, www.coyote.com.py.
Several dance floors and bars, affluent crowd, see website for other events in different locations including Ciudad del Este and San Bernardino. Recommended.

Face's
Av Mcal López 2585 (technically in Fernando de la Mora), T021-671421/672768, www.faces.com.py. Also in Ciudad del Este.
Largest club in Paraguay, shows nightly.

Glam
Av San Martin 1155 y Agustín Barrios, T021-331905, www.glam.com.py.
Along with Coyote and Face's (see above), one of Asunción's most popular clubs. Thu, Fri and Sat.

Trauma
*25 de Mayo 760 y Antequera y Tacuary,
T981-204020.*
Gay/transvestite/mixed, Fri, Sat, 2300.

Cinema and theatre
See newspapers for films, performances
of concerts, plays and ballets. For online
listings, check **ABC Digital** (www.abc.
com.py), **Última Hora** (www.ultimahora.
com) and **La Nación** (www.lanacion.
com.py). See also *Asunción Viva*, above,
and the monthly *Asunción Quick Guide*
(www.quickguide.com.py). Cinema
admission US$5 (Wed and matinées half
price). Most shopping malls have modern
cinemas; see Shopping centres, below.
For the **Teatro Municipal**, see above.
Various cultural centres also put on films,
theatrical productions and events:
Alianza Francesa, *Estigarribia 1039
y Estados Unidos, T021-210503, http://
alianzafrancesapy.blogspot.com.*
**Centro Cultural Paraguayo
Americano**, *España 352 entre Brasil y
Estados Unidos, T021224831,
www.ccpa.edu.py.*
Centro Paraguayo-Japonés, *Av Julio
Corea y Domingo Portillo, T021-607277,
www.centroparaguayojapones.
blogspot.com.*
Goethe-Zentrum Asunción, *Juan de
Salazar 310 y Artigas, T021-226242,
www.goethe.de/ins/pa/asu.*

2 weeks in **Jul**, **Expo**, an annual trade
show at Mariano Roque Alonso,
Km 14.5 on the Trans-Chaco Highway.
The biggest fair in the country with
local and international exhibitors.
Packed at weekends. Bus from centre
takes 30 mins.

Bookshops
English-language books are expensive
throughout Paraguay.
'Books', *at Shopping del Sol, T021-611730,
and Mcal López 3971, also opposite Villa
Morra shopping centre, T021-603722,
www.libreriabooks.com.* Very good for
English books, new titles and classics.
El Lector, *San Martín y Austria, T021-
610639, www.ellector.com.py.* Has a
selection of foreign material and a range
of its own titles on Paraguay. Also has
café and internet connection.

> **Tip...**
>
> Check the quality of all handicrafts
> carefully; in the city, lower prices
> usually mean lower quality. Many
> leading tourist shops offer up to 15%
> discount for cash; many others will not
> accept credit cards, so ask even if there
> are signs in window saying they do.

Crafts
For leather goods there are several
places on Colón and on Montevideo
including: **Boutique Irene**, *No 463*;
Boutique del Cuero, *No 329*; and **Galería
Colón 185**, recommended. Also **La Casa
del Portafolio**, *Av Palma 302, T021-492431.*
Artes de Madera, *Ayolas 222.* Wooden
articles and carvings.
Casa Overall 1, *Estigarribia y Caballero,
T021-448657.* Good selection. Also **No 2**,
25 de Mayo y Caballero, T021-447891.
Casa Vera, *Estigarribia 470, T021-445868,
www.casavera.com.py.* For Paraguayan
leatherwork, cheap and very good.
Doña Miky, *O'Leary 215 y Pres Franco.*
Recommended.
Folklore, *Estigarribia e Iturbe, T021-494360.*
Good for music and woodcarvings.

Victoria, Arte Artesanía, *Iturbe y Ayala,
T021-450148*. Interesting selection
of wood carvings, ceramics, etc.
Recommended.

La Recova, *near the waterfront*.
Asunción's general-purpose market
has served as an open-air and covered
emporium for all manner of handicrafts
and traditional goods (including better-
grade hammocks, leather and silver
products) for more than 150 years. It takes
some searching to find the best deals, but
the markets here are endlessly colourful
and vibrant, with wares usually cheaper
than in Plaza Libertad or along Av Palma.

Markets

Mercado Cuatro, *in the blocks bounded
by Pettirossi, Perú and Av Dr Francia*.
A huge daily market selling food,
clothing, electrical items, DVDs, CDs,
jewellery, toys, is a great place to visit.
Good, cheap Chinese restaurants nearby.
Shopping Mariscal López *(see below)*.
Has a fruit and veg market, Tue, in the car
park, and a small plant/flower market,
including orchids, Wed, at the entrance.

Shopping centres

Asunción has a number of modern
Shopping Malls with shops, ATMs,
cafés, supermarkets, cinemas and food
halls all under one a/c roof. Most also
offer Wi-Fi coverage. In the centre is
Mall Excelsior (Chile y Manduvirá,
T021-443015, www.mallexcelsior.com).
Shopping Villa Morra (Av Mcal López
y San Roque González, T021-603050,
www.svm.com.py). **Shopping Mariscal
López** (Quesada 5050 y Charles de
Gaulle, behind Shopping Villa Morra,
T021-611272, www.mariscallopez.com.
py). **Shopping del Sol** (Av Aviadores de
Chaco y D F de González, T021-611780,
www.delsol.com.py).

Football

Asunción (technically nextdoor Luque)
is the permanent home of the **South
American Football Confederation,
CONMEBOL** (www.conmebol.com),
on the autopista heading towards the
airport, opposite Ñu Guazú Park. This
imposing building with its striking
'football' fountain houses offices, a hall
of fame, extensive football library and a
new museum with interactive exhibits,
T021-494628 in advance for visits. See
also **Asociación Paraguaya de Futbol**
(www.apf.org.py).
Estadio Defensores del Chaco,
*Mayor Martínez 1393 y Alejo García,
T021-480120*. Is the national stadium,
hosting international, cup and
major club matches.

Horse riding

Club Hípico Paraguayo, *Av Eusebio
Ayala y Benjamín Aceval, Barrio San Jorge
Mariano Roque Alonso, T021-756148*.
Actually 9 different athletic clubs in one;
scene of many Asunción society events.
Members club (US$55 per month but
daily rates available) open to the public.
Friendly and helpful.

Language schools

Idipar (Idiomas en Paraguay),
*Manduvirá 963, T021-447896, www.idipar.
net*. Offers courses in Spanish or Guaraní.
Private or group lessons available,
also offers accommodation with local
families and volunteer opportunities.
Good standard.
IPEE, *Lugano 790 y Ayolas, T021-447482*.
Spanish or Guaraní, in individual or
group classes. Recommended.
One2One, *Cecilio da Silva 980, T021-
613507, www.one2one.com.py*. Good for

immersion or business Spanish (as well as other languages).

Nature and rural tourism
See boxes, pages 42 and 60.

Tour operators
Many agencies offer day tours of the **Circuito de Oro** or **Camino Franciscano** (from US$50), with the possibility of different stops for each agency, so ask in advance which locations are included on the itinerary. Trips to local estancias, Encarnación and the former Jesuit missions, Itaipú and Iguazú or the Chaco region are all offered as 1-, 2- or 4-day tours. Most agencies will also provide personalized itineraries on request. Many more city tours, especially those focusing on architecture and culture, are also now available. For more information contact **Senatur** or the **Paraguayan Association of Travel Agencies and Tourism (ASATUR)** (Juan O'Leary 650, p 1, T021-494728, www.asatur.org.py). Also, Paraguay's official national cultural organ, the Cabildo (see page 139), offers several options for itineraries throughout the country and capital.

Canadá Viajes, *Rep de Colombia 1061, T021-211192, www.canadaviajes.com.py.* Good Asunción and Chaco tours.

Cuñataí, *at Sporting Club of Puerto Sajonia, T021-420375.* Boat tours of Asunción and Río Paraguay, departures Sun, 1700, 140-people capacity.

Inter Tours and Martín Travel, *Perú 436 y España, T021-211747, www.intertours.com.py/www.martintravel.com.py.* One of Paraguay's biggest full-service tour agencies. Tours to Chaco, Iguazú and Jesuit missions. Highly recommended.

Menno Travel, *Rep de Colombia 1042 entre Brasil y EEUU, T021-493504, mennotra@tigo. com.py.* German spoken.

Time Tours, *Asunción Super Centro, loc 197, T021-449737, info@timetours.com.py.* Fluent English, runs Camino Franciscano tours. Recommended.

Vips Tour, *México 782 entre Fulgencio R Moreno y Herrera, T021-441199, also at Senador Long 790 y Tte Vera, T021-615920, www.vipstour.com.* Asunción, estancia and Chaco tours.

Guides
Oscar Daniel González, *T981-21 7082, osgonzaga1@hotmail.com.* Private tours of the Circuito de Oro, US$70 pp per day, in Spanish.

Air
Silvio Pettirossi Airport, T021-645600. Several agencies have desks where you can book a taxi to your hotel, up to US$30. Bus 30 goes every 15 mins between the red bus stop outside the airport and Plaza de los Héroes, US$1, difficult with luggage. Minibus service from your hotel to airport run by **Tropical**, T021-424486, book in advance, US$2.70 (minimum 2 passengers, or pay for 2). The terminal has a tourist office (free city map and hotel information), bank (turn right as you leave customs – better rates in town), post office (0800-1800), handicraft shop (good quality, expensive), restaurant and several travel agencies who arrange hotel bookings and change money (very poor rates). Left luggage US$5 per day per item.

Bus
Local   Journeys within greater Asunción US$0.75. Buses can be busy at rush hours. Turnstiles are awkward for large backpacks. Keep your ticket for inspection until you leave bus.

Long distance The Terminal de Omnibus, TOA, is south of the centre at República Argentina y Fernando de la Mora, T021-551740, www.mca.gov. py/toa.htm. Local bus No 8 is the only direct one from Oliva, which goes via Cerro Corá and Av Brasil from the centre, and stops on the opposite side of Av F de la Mora to the terminal, US$0.75. From the terminal to the centre it goes via Brasil, FR Moreno, Antequera, Plaza Uruguaya and E Ayala. Get out between Chile and Alberdi for Plaza de los Héroes. Other buses, eg No 31, follow more circuitous routes. Taxi to/from centre, recommended if you have luggage, US$8-10, journey time depends on the amount of traffic, about 45 mins. The terminal has a bus information desk, free city/country map, restaurant (quite good), café, *casas de cambio* (poor rates), ATM, post office, phone booths and shops. There are many touts for bus companies at the terminal. Allow yourself time to choose the company you want and don't be tricked into buying the wrong ticket. Better companies include **Nuestra Señora de la Asunción**, T021-289 1000, www. nsa.com.py, has booking office at main terminal and at Mariscal Estigarribia y Antequera, off Plaza Uruguaya (mainly for its tours), and at Benjamín Constant 984, opposite Aduanas. Some of its buses are direct, ie they don't stop everywhere and anywhere. **RYSA**, T021-557201/551601, www.rysa.com.py, has a booking office at Ayala y Antequera by Plaza Uruguaya. Also recommended are **La Ovetense** (T021-551737), **Nasa-Golondrina** (T021-551731) for domestic destinations. Bus company offices are on the top floor of the terminal. Local departures, including for Yaguarón and Paraguarí, are boarded from the basement. Bus fares within Paraguay are given under destinations, also available on TOA's website. Note that all journey times are approximate.

To Argentina There is a road north from Asunción (passing the Jardín Botánico on Primer Presidente) to a concrete arch span bridge (Puente Remanso – US$1.25 toll, pedestrian walkway on upstream side, 20 mins to cross) which leads to the border at Puerto Falcón (about 40 km) and then to **Clorinda** in Argentina. The border is open 24 hrs; local services are run by **Empresa Falcón** to **Puerto Falcón**: US$1.25, every hr, last bus from Falcón to the centre of Asunción 1830; from Falcón to **Clorinda** costs US$0.75, but direct from Asunción to Clorinda is US$1. **Note** Buses don't wait for you to go through formalities: if you cannot process in time, wait for the same company's next bus and present ticket, or buy a new ticket.

Buses to **Buenos Aires** (18 hrs) daily, many companies, via Rosario and Santa Fe (fares range from US$30-65). To **Resistencia** and **Corrientes**, many daily, US$9.50 to Resistencia, US$11 to Corrientes; many drug searches on this road. To **Salta**, take a bus to **Resistencia**, then change to **Flecha** or **La Veloz del Norte**, or take a bus on the route through the Chaco, as below.

To Brazil Many Paraguayan buses advertise that they go to destinations in Brazil, when, in fact you have to change buses and book again at the border. Services to **Campo Grande** and **Corumbá** via Pedro Juan Caballero and Ponta Porã do not stop for immigration formalities. Check all details carefully. **Nuestra Señora de la Asunción** and others, and the Brazilian company **Pluma**

(T021-551196, www.pluma.com.br) have direct services via Ciudad del Este to **Foz do Iguaçu** (Brazil), US$25-30, 5-6 hrs. To **Curitiba**, with **Pluma** and others, daily, 15½ hrs, US$45. To **Florianópolis**, **Pluma** and **Catarinense**, US$60 (T021-551738, www.catarinense.net), you may have to change in Cascavel. To **Porto Alegre**, Uneleste (T021-442679), Tue, Thu, US$60. To **São Paulo**, **Pluma**, **Sol** and **Brújula**, 20 hrs, US$45-70. **Pluma** to **Rio de Janeiro**, US$80 (not Sat); **Transcontinental** (T021-557369) to **Brasília** 3 a week, US$100.

To Bolivia Via the Chaco, to Santa Cruz, **Yacyretá**, T021-551725, Mon, Wed, Fri, and Sat at 2030, **Pycazú**, T021-555235, Thu, Sat 2100, **Palma Loma**, T021-558196, and **Río Paraguay**, T021-555958. All fares from US$40. All buses normally travel via Mariscal Estigarribia, for Paraguayan immigration where foreigners must get an exit stamp; La Patria; Infante Rivarola at the border (no stamps are given here); Ibibobo, for Bolivian immigration; and Villamontes. From here buses go either to Yacuiba for Argentina (Pocitos and on to Salta on Ruta 54), or direct to Santa Cruz. Advertised as 21 hrs, the trip can take 2 days to Santa Cruz if the bus breaks down. Some food provided on both Salta and Santa Cruz routes, but take your own, plus extra water just in case; also take toilet paper. The buses can be very crowded. In summer the route can be very hot and dusty, but in winter, it can be cold at night.

Unless specifically advertised (eg Nasa–Golondrina), buses to Bolivia do not go through Filadelfia or the other Mennonite colonies, so take a local service from Asunción (see page 35). After visiting the Chaco, you can usually get on a Bolivia-bound bus in Mariscal Estigarribia, where the bus companies have agents (see page 116), but enquire in advance with their offices in Asunción.

Car hire

Fast Rent a Car, Prof Chávez 1276 y Santa Rosa, T021-605462, www.fastrentacar.com.py. Good, helpful. Also other companies at the airport. Note that all Paraguayan car hire agencies require payment in US dollars as well as a deposit secured by a credit card of between US$500-1000.

Taxi

Taxi meters start at US$1.15 and rise in US$0.10 increments. There is a late night surcharge after 2200 to 0500. There are many taxi ranks throughout the city. Taxis can either be hailed or call **Radiotaxi** (recommended), T021-550116/311080.

River

A small launch leaves from the pier at the bottom of Montevideo to **Chaco-i**, a strip of land between the Ríos Paraguay and Pilcomayo (no facilities), US$0.75 each way. Also across the river is the **Mbiguá Club** (rather run down), Facebook: Club-Mbigua-Oficial, boat fare US$4.50. The Argentine town of Clorinda is just the other side of the Pilcomayo, but there are no ferries or immigration for crossing here.

For boat travel to **Concepción**, see under Concepción, Transport, page 99.

Train

At the time of writing, no tourist steam trains were running from Asunción.

South of Asunción: Ruta 1

Ruta 1 and Ruta 8 run south and east to the southern Paraneña (the country's breadbasket and home to its gauchos) and the former Jesuit missions – two of which are now World Heritage Sites. The roads then merge at Coronel Bogado before reaching the Río Paraguay in Encarnación, an increasingly popular destination for the country's fledgling water tourism sector and a crossing point for travel to Argentina.

There are multiple approaches to exploring this area, and the two best-known routes, the Circuito de Oro and the Camino Franciscano (see pages 26 and 27), overlap in places. Unless bound to a specific itinerary arranged by a tour operator, the easiest way to make the most of this region is simply to take one of the three main *rutas* and follow it from one end (usually Asunción) to the other.

Best for
Arts and crafts ▪ Religious architecture ▪ Wildlife

centre for arts and crafts with workshops and a museum

Paraguay's Ruta 1 begins just outside Asunción's city limits in San Lorenzo (see page 26) at the intersection of Avenida Mcal F S López and Avenida Mariscal Estigarribia. The first few kilometres are mostly urban landscape. At Km 23 is the town of Juan Augusto Saldívar, the country's centre for tangerine production. At the fork in the road in the section of town called Tres Bocas (marked) bear right.

Itá

At Km 37, Itá (population 17,469) is Paraguay's second-oldest town, settled as a Franciscan mission in 1539. It is famous for rustic pottery, but also sells wood, leather and textile items including hammocks and exquisite cloth dolls.

At the town's entrance you can visit the workshop of **Doña Rosa Brítez** ① *Ruta 1, entre San Lorenzo y Guarambare, T971-121126*, a local ceramics artist and Paraguay's most famous artisan, of such stature that she was recognized by UNESCO. For information on her *taller* (which functions under the guidance of her children), see www.portalguarani.com/724_rosa_britez.html. Approaching the centre, there is a highly regarded *artesanía*, the **Centro de Artesanos y Pequeñas Industrias de la Ciudad de Itá** ① *Gral Díaz y Cerro Corá, T0224-632057, Mon-Fri 0730-1730, free*; prices here are usually better than in Asunción.

Just before the main plaza, a left-hand turn at the traffic signal and 3 km up the road leads to the **Casa Museo Arte en Barro** ① *Gral Marcial Samaniego, T971-245101, Mon-Fri 0700-1800, free*, another art centre, this time a house and museum featuring the pottery of mother and daughter artists, Juana Marta Rodas and Julia Isídrez. Visitors are usually met at the door by either mother or daughter and given a leisurely tour and of course a cup of mate.

Itá's pretty Franciscan mission church, **San Blas** ① *San Blas entre Carlos A López y Enrique Doldán Ibieta, T0224-632291*, is on the plaza. Built in 1698, it is honoured both nationally and internationally as an architectural and historic patrimony.

In keeping with its reputation as a centre for traditional crafts, Itá has another interesting taller/quasi-museum, the **Museo Ñande Ypycué** ① *Tte Rojas Silva y Gral Caballero 1010, http://circuitossolidarios.org/museo-nande-ypycue, free*, featuring wonderful carvings made by the late Doña Mercedes de Servín. It is now maintained by her niece, who preserves the art form and is a recognized maestra in her own right. The town has a lagoon which is reputed never to dry up.

Yaguarón

an unusual church and a museum on Paraguay's first dictator

Founded in 1539, Yaguarón (Km 48, population 8926) was a key centre of the Franciscan missions in colonial times.

At the centre of the town, marooned on an island of green, mown grass, stands the church of **San Buenaventura** ① *daily 0700-1200 and 1400-1800*, with its external belltower. The simplicity and symmetry of the exterior is matched by the ornate carvings and paintings of the interior. The tints, made by the *indígenas* from local plants, are still bright on the woodcarvings and the angels have Guaraní faces. The church is quite unusual from an architectural perspective, as the Franciscans, unlike their Jesuit counterparts, did not normally build such sophisticated *templos*, but favoured instead more simple structures. Built in Hispano-Guaraní baroque style by the Franciscans between 1640 and 1775, it was reconstructed in 1885 and renovated in the late 20th century. Stations of the Cross behind the village lead to a good view of the surroundings.

Not to be missed is the **Museo Dr José Gaspar Rodríguez de Francia** ⓘ *leaving the church, 500 m down the road to your left, Pirayú 325, T0533-177797, www.portalguarani.com (under 'Museums and cultural centres'), Mon-Fri 0730-1200 and 1400-1800, free guided tour in Spanish*, with artefacts from the life of Paraguay's first dictator, the bizarre 'El Supremo', plus paintings and artefacts from the 18th century. The single-storey adobe building with bamboo ceilings and tiled roof belonged to Francia's father.

There are a few basic hotels ($) and buses from Asunción run every 15 minutes, US$0.75. The town's patronal feast of **San Buenaventura**, is in mid-July. At the festival for **San Roque** (16 August, first Sunday in September) music is provided by the Banda Peteke Peteke, a unique group that plays the mimby flute and two small drums.

Outside town, the **Cerro Yaguarón**, which has a nice view of the surrounding countryside, is famous as the site of centuries-old Good Friday processions. Owing to its terrain, Yaguarón has the dubious distinction of having one of the coldest winter climates in Paraguay.

Pirayú

From the centre of Yaguarón, to the immediate left of the church, take the Ruta Yaguaron–Pirayú which leads to the pleasant town of Pirayú, 10 km away. Much of the colonial centre is still preserved and the town has a now-closed railway depot dating from 1860. Just outside the town is the lovely Cascada Arroyo Madama, a wonderful spot for an al fresco lunch and supposedly much frequented by Francisco Solano López' mistress Eliza Lynch. To return to Asunción from Pirayú, continue north on this same road for 12.5 km until reaching Ypacaraí, where you can take Ruta 2 back to the capital.

Paraguarí and around

historic towns, great scenery, and an excellent eco-park

Founded in 1775 and located at Km 63, Paraguarí (population 12,661) is the usual northern entrance to the mission area, at the foot of a range of hills. Now relegated to the history books, the town was the site of the Battle of Paraguarí in 1811, a decisive engagement in the war for preserving Paraguayan independence against encroaching Argentine troops. Its restored church has two bell towers, separate from the main structure. Buses between Asunción and Encarnación stop here.

One kilometre from the centre, on the site of a former Jesuit estancia (originally the largest of all the estancias in colonial Paraguay), is an interesting artillery museum, the **Museo Histórico Gral Enrique Duarte Alder de la Artillería** ① *T0531-432274, www.portalguarani.com (under 'Museums and cultural centres'), free,* but prior permission to visit is required as it is still military property, now part of a nearby military base, with cannons and artefacts from the Chaco War. Its chapel holds a remarkable statue of Santa Bárbara, which is brought out on her feast day (4 December). In the same complex you can stroll to the top of Cerro Peró for views from the cross on top. More challenging is a one-hour climb through dense forest to the summit of **Cerro Jhu** (officially known as Cerro Mbatoví but rarely called that, and not to be confused with the Eco Reserva Mbatoví, see below); ask for directions to the cerro anywhere in Barrio San Miguel behind the abandoned train station. Paraguarí retains many customs from its founding and is considered Paraguay's capital of bullfighting. Each year on 21 December the town goes all out for its patronal feast of St Thomas and bullfights (*toro moñaroha* in Guaraní) are held. Paraguarí is also well known for its watermelons, which are best purchased at the **Frutería Paraguarí** immediately after the Puma petrol station on Ruta 1 as it approaches the centre.

Eco Reserva Mbatoví

The **Eco Reserva Mbatoví** ① *www.mbatovi.com.py,* is 10 km northeast of Paraguarí on the Ruta Paraguari–Piribebuy and well worth a detour. It is without doubt the finest eco-adventure park in the country and a rare example of a successful private reserve that is easily accessed by car. The cost is US$35 per person for non-Paraguayans and includes a three-hour guided interpretive tour. Rappelling, hiking and zip-lining are optional activities. The reserve is stunningly beautiful, but its ecosystem is fragile; visitor numbers are at the discretion of the proprietors (a husband and wife who are dedicated preservationists) and reservations must be made a day in advance (T021-444844 from Asunción or T971-659820; payment made by bank transfer only, no cash).

Chololó

Northeast from Paraguarí 15 km (or 5 km from the Eco Reserva Mbatoví; take Ruta Paraguari–Piribebuy and turn left 1.5 km after leaving Mbatoví; bus US$1) is Chololó, with a small but attractive series of waterfalls and rapids with bathing facilities and walkways, mainly visited in the summer.

Sapucai

Some 23 km east of Paraguarí on Ruta Paraguari–Villarrica, Sapucai (population 2354) was until recently the terminus of the tourist train from Asunción. It still houses the antique **locomotives' workshops** ① *just outside of the entrance to town, Mon-Fri,* which are currently being restored. In the 'train cemetery' (similar to the much better-known one in Uyuni, Bolivia) you can see old, abandoned wood-burning steam locomotives. There is also a small museum attached (T0539-263218). Tour operators like to point out that it is the world's last steam locomotive

ON THE ROAD

Rural tourism

Turismo rural is an enjoyable way to visit the country and get a feel for a Paraguayan way of life that revolves around agriculture and ranching. It is not as advanced as rural tourism in Argentina, Chile or Uruguay, amenities are modest and there is little concerted promotion of estancias, but the sector is slowly growing in Paraguay, particularly in the southeast (in Paraguarí, Caaguazú, Guairá and Caazapá departments) and to the east and northeast of Asunción (in Cordillera and San Pedro departments).

The Touring y Automóvil Club Paraguayo (TACPy) (25 de Mayo y Brasíl, p 2, T021-210550, www.tacpy.com.py), is a potential source of information on rural tourism, although it now focuses primarily upon 3 regions: mission tours (to Villa Florida, San Ignacio Guazú, Santa María de Fe and Santiago Apóstol); the Alto Paraná (including Itaipú, the Salto de Monday falls and Ciudad del Este); and Guairá (essentially the city of Villarrica).

Thanks to increased government support for its mission, however, the Paraguayan Rural Tourism Association (APATUR), Don Bosco 881, T021-497028, http://turismorural.org.py, is taking over this role. With advance notice, it can help organize visits to ranches and farms throughout the country's more accessible regions (there is a list on the website).

Visitors experience living on a ranch, can participate in a variety of activities, and enjoy typical food, horse riding, photo safaris and nature watching. One-day tour prices are about US$60-95 per person including accommodation, food and drink (not alcohol). All the ranches promoted by APATUR supposedly have good facilities, although there is as yet no accepted standardization. Transport to and from these ranches from Asunción is sometimes included in the package. See also the Ministry of Tourism (Senatur) website, www.senatur.gov.py, Turismo rural page, under Sentir la naturaleza, for a list of ranches that welcome tourists. All visits should be arranged at least one week in advance and confirmed prior to leaving Asunción.

repair shop (although travellers not fascinated by steam locomotives may want to give it a miss). You can get there by bus from Asunción in three hours (0530 and 1310). Close by is Paraguay's first viaduct, constructed by English engineers in 1897. The neighbourhood in which they lived is still known as **Villa Inglesa** and has several original houses constructed in late Victorian style. There are also some *hospedajes* (all $) in town. Sapucai is nowadays known as a centre of agricultural production, particularly alfalfa, cane sugar, cotton and honey. For information on Sapucai, see www.sapucai.net.

Carapeguá

The town of Carapeguá (population 6825), at Km 84, may not have much to recommend itself to the traveller (there's a friendly, basic *hospedaje* on the main street; blankets and hammocks to rent along the main road, or buy your own, made locally and cheaper than elsewhere), but its environs offer excellent scenery. After a left-hand turn onto Ruta Carapeguá–Acahay at the Esso petrol station on Ruta 1, a 22-km drive leads to the 560-m **Cerro Acahay**, which has wonderful far-reaching views and is accessible by a well-marked road. For information on Carapeguá, see http://carapegua.blogspot.com.

Parque Nacional Lago Ypoá

If staying on Ruta 1 instead, pass through the centre of Carapeguá and signs for Lago Ypoá National Park will appear on the right. The 100,000-ha park consists mostly of marshes, islands, mountains and lakes. In 1995 it was declared a 'Wetland of International Importance' and made a Ramsar Site. There are a number of small picturesque communities in the area, and multiple access routes, some of which are private; ask in town. The closest to Ruta 1 is made by all-terrain vehicle from the town of **San Roque González de Santa Cruz**, 14 km south of Carapeguá (Km 96 on Ruta 1).

Quiíndy

Usually overlooked, the idyllic town of Quiíndy (population 16,074), at Km 103 is inevitably passed through by travellers en route to Ybycuí to the east or Caapucú to the south. It's worth a stop, however, because of its beautiful scenery and the streams and rivers that run through the town. Its thoroughly modern Iglesia San Lorenzo was built on the foundations of an earlier Franciscan mission church dating from the 16th century. Quiíndy, somewhat bizarrely, is known as the country's centre for the manufacture of leather and plastic balls.

Listings Paraguarí and around

Restaurants

La Frutería
Ruta 1, Km 61, T0531-432406, about 2.5 km before the town.
Wide selection of fruit, outdoor seating and a restaurant serving *empanadas*, hamburgers, beer, fruit salad.
Highly recommended.

Transport

Bus City buses leave from lower level of the Asunción terminal every 15 mins throughout the day, but much faster to take an Encarnación-bound bus from the upper level, same fare US$1.

virgin rainforest, hiking trails, waterfalls and butterflies

There are two branch roads from Ruta 1 to reach this national park, one of Paraguay's most accessible. The first, from Carapeguá, is made by turning right at the Esso petrol station onto Ruta Carapegua–Acahay to Acahay (22 km), from Acahay to Ybycuí (another 17 km), then to the Parque Nacional Ybycuí (another 26 km). Alternatively, access it from Quiíndy, along Ruta Quiíndy–Ybycuí (49 km).

The **park** ⓘ *www.salvemoslos.com.py/pny.htm, 0800-1700. For camping get a permit from the Secretaría del Ambiente, Madame Lynch 3500, in Asunción; see National parks, page 60*, is one of the few remaining strands of Atlantic forest in eastern Paraguay. Founded in 1973, it protects 5000 ha of virgin forest and offers good walks (guides available), a beautiful campsite and lots of waterfalls. At the entrance is a well-set-out park and museum, plus the reconstructed remains of the country's first iron foundry (La Rosada). The park can get crowded on Sundays but is mostly deserted the rest of the week. The only shops (apart from a small one at the entrance selling drinks, eggs, etc, and a good T-shirt stall which helps support the park) are at **Ybycuí**, 43 km northwest.

Essential Ybycuí

Finding your feet

Bus There are 2 per day, 1000 and 1600 from **Ybycuí**, US$1.25, take bus going to the Mbocaya Pucú colony that stops in front of the park entrance. From **Asunción** take a bus to Acahay, **Transportes Emilio Cabrera**, 8 daily and change, or bus to Ybycuí, 0630, US$2.75

Where to stay

$$$ Estancia Santa Clara
Km 141, Ruta 1, Caapucú, T021-605729, www.estancia santaclara.com.py.
Tourism farm offering rural activites in a beautiful setting between Paraguarí and San Ignacio Guazú, full board or visit for the day (mini-zoo). Reserve in advance.

$$ Hotel Pytyu'u Renda
Av General Caballero 509 y Quyquyho, Ybycuí, T0534-226364.
Good food, cooking facilities.

Caapucú

Located at Km 141 (32 km from Quiíndy), the tiny town of Caapucú (population 2242) makes for an interesting stop for several reasons. Its **Museo Casa Oratorio Cabañas** ⓘ *on Ruta 1, 12 km south of town, T971-359295, www.portalguarani.com (under 'Museums and cultural centres'), Tue-Sat 0900-1600*, is one of the oldest buildings still surviving in its original form anywhere in the country, having been built sometime around 1690. Also known as the *antigua alquería* (old farmhouse), the building has an interesting, even tragic, history. Originally the main house of an extensive estancia, in 1724 it served as headquarters for Paraguay's first freedom fighter, José de Antequera, executed soon after. The house was later inhabited by Manuel Belgrano in 1811 as he attempted to liberate Paraguay from Spain and annex it to Argentina, but he was forced to abandon it and return ignominiously to Argentina. If this weren't enough, the property in 1828 was deeded by 'El Supremo' Francia,

Paraguay's paranoid dictator, to a cousin who was forced to barricade himself in the house when his uncle turned against him. The next owner fared no better and was left to starve in the house by Francia. His descendants granted the house to the government in 1973 on the condition that it be turned into a museum, whereupon it was immediately plundered by vandals and treasure seekers who nearly destroyed the edifice. It has now been more or less restored to its original colonial glory.

Caapucú has preserved a good number of colonial-era houses and the town is attractive on the whole. One of them, the **Casa Antigua Familia Stewart** ① *turn left 3 blocks past main plaza, T981-836247*, whose architecture resembles a miniature castle, has been turned into a museum that exhibits artifacts from that era. The family emigrated from England when William Stewart was asked to serve as the doctor of President Francisco Solano Lopéz, and its descendants still live in the vicinity.

Caapucú has several very attractive tourist spots, and is ideal as a base for day trips to other recreational places such as Lago Ypoa-Guazú, where there is good fishing. The nearby resort of Paso Ybycuí is quite beautiful and has facilities for camping and sports. In town, informal tours of local *cerros*, such as Charorá, Virgen, Yaguarete-Cuá, Tarumá, Mariño, Villalba, Arayhú and Mbocayá can be arranged. Ask at the **municipalidad** ① *T0535-280279, caapucu@contratacíonesparaguay.gov. py, Mon-Fri 0700-1300*, off the plaza.

Villa Florida

Ruta 1 continues through Villa Florida (population 2930) at Km 162, on the banks of the Río Tebicuary, a tributary of the Río Paraguay to the west. As with Paraguarí to the north, Villa Florida played an important although now-forgotten role in Paraguay's struggle for independence, serving as the strategic base of General Manuel Atanasio Cabañas. It's a popular spot with Paraguayans in January and February for its sandy beaches. The fishing here used to be first-rate but stocks are now depleted and the town is attempting to promote other water sports.

Buses from Asunción and Encarnación stop at Villa Florida. The **Hotel Nacional de Villa Florida** ($$, T083-240207) and the Touring y Automóvil Club's **Hotel-Parador Villa Florida** (Km 156, T083-40205, www.tacpy.com.py) would both make a convenient stopover. There are several other hotels in the $$-$ range, all near the banks of the river and advertising beaches and air-conditioning. For more information on the town, see http://villafloridalaweb.blogspot.com.

San Juan Bautista

At Km 196, San Juan Bautista (population 18,441), the gateway to the Jesuit missions to the south, comes into view. Apart from its several Catholic institutions (it is the diocesan seat of the region), it is best known for its agricultural products and as the birthplace of Agustín Pío Barrios, Paraguay's best-known guitarist, considered by some the greatest of all time. His house is now the **Casa y Museo Mangoré** ① *Presidente Franco y República Argentina, T995-353070*. The town recently created a cultural centre, the Centro Cultural Ka'avo, to encourage the region's Jesuit and Guaraní traditions. Several events are sponsored throughout the year. For information, ask at the church on the beautiful Plaza Mariscal Estigarribia, where there is free Wi-Fi. The town's patronal feast is on 24 June and is famous for serving local delicacies (many of indigenous origin). There are several modest hotels ($$-$) along Ruta 1 and many inexpensive restaurants. For information on San Juan Baustista, see http://misiones.gov.py/san-juan-bautista.

★Jesuit missions

traditional ex-mission towns and a museum not to be missed

Eight *reducciones* remain in Paraguay in varying states of repair and two (La Santísima Trinidad de Paraná and Jesús de Tavarangue, page 53) have been inscribed as UNESCO World Heritage Sites, with two others, San Ignacio Guazú and San Cosme y Damián, also of importance.

San Ignacio Guazú and around

Some 32 km south of San Juan Bautista, at Km 226 at the intersection of Rutas 1 and 4, San Ignacio Guazú (population 17,422) is a delightful town on the site of a former Jesuit *reducción* (*guazú* means 'big' in Guaraní). Several typical Hispano-Guaraní buildings survive in various states of preservation. Each Sunday night at 2000 a folklore festival and light show is held in the central plaza (free; very local, "fabulous"). The **Museo Jesuítico** ① *also known as Museo Diocesano de Arte de las Reducciones Jesuíticas, Av San Roque González de Santa Cruz y Cerro Corá, T0782-232223, www.portalguarani.com (under 'Museums and cultural centres'), daily 0800-1130, 1400-1730, US$1; for guided tours, T975-631352 and T985-835966,* housed in the former Jesuit art workshop across from the parish offices, reputedly the oldest surviving civil building in Paraguay, contains a major collection of Guaraní art and sculpture from the missionary period. It is organized into four rooms themed 'Creation', 'Redemption', 'Christ in the Church' and 'History of the Jesuits'. Among other objects of cultural value are rare sculptures carved in polychrome wood, period maps of the first Jesuit mission in Paraguay, and photographs of the original church (taken before its restoration). The attendant is very knowledgeable. Photos are not allowed. One block over is the **Museo Histórico Sembranza de Héroes** ① *Iturbe y Av San Roque González de Santa Cruz, T975-631352, www.portalguarani.com (under*

Essential Jesuit missions

Getting around

Numerous Asunción- and Encarnación-based tour operators offer tours of these missions. Santiago-based **Emitur** ① *T0782-20286, emitur.misiones@gmail.com,* offers excellent area tours and also visits to local ranches. Also see **Cámara Paraguaya de Turismo de las Misiones Jesuíticas** ① *Mariscal Estigarribia 1031 y Curupayty, Encarnación, T071-205021, rutajesuiticapy@hotmail.com.* For information on the La Santísima Trinidad de Paraná and Jesús de Tavarangue ex-missions themselves, see http://whc.unesco.org/en/list/648. Caution is advised after 2200 and in market areas.

'Museums and cultural centres'), Mon-Fri 0700-1200, 1300-1700, free, with displays on the Chaco War and native Guaraní ceramics.

Pilar
Before continuing along Ruta 1 to the east, towards the centre of town there is a turning to the right at the Puma service station which heads to **Pilar** (population 31,612; hotels in **$$-$** range), 132 km to the west on Ruta 4, on the banks of the Río Paraguay. Capital of Ñeembucú district, the town is known for its fishing festival (one of the largest in South America is held during Holy Week), textile manufacturing (Pilar's fabrics are considered the best in Paraguay) and historic **Cabildo de Pilar** ⓘ *T086-223078, 14 de mayo y Mcal F S López, www.cultura.gov.py (under 'Museos del Paraguay'), Mon-Fri 0730-1100 and 1400-1700; Sat 0900-1600, free.* In early January the town's **Fiesta Hawaiana** attracts tens of thousands of visitors. Pilar is unique in the country for having a successful youth tourism initiative. This area saw many bloody battles during the War of the Triple Alliance.

Also of interest is **Humaitá** (40 km to the south on Ruta 4), with the Basílica de Nuestra Señora de Pilar, the old church of San Carlos; **Paso de Patria** (22 km further south); **Curupayty** and other historic battle sites.

Santa María de Fe
From San Ignacio Guazú, the quintessential ex-mission town of Santa María de Fe is 3.5 km northeast, first along Ruta 1 and then a left onto a paved road (marked), followed for another 10.5 km. Established in its current location in 1669, the **Museo Jesuítico de Santa María de Fe** ⓘ *on the main plaza, T0781-283332, www.portalguarani.com (under 'Museums and cultural centres'), Tue-Sun 0830-1130, 1330-1700, US$1, photos allowed,* is housed in an original *casa de indios* (indigenous house). Other exhibits are in restored mission buildings and contain more than 60 Guaraní sculptures. The complex is considered one of the country's finest museums for mission art and of all the Jesuit museums in the country, this one is not to be missed. The modern church has a lovely altarpiece of the Virgin and Child (the key is kept at a house on the opposite side of the plaza; ask at the museum during

the day only). There is also the **Santa María Cooperative and Educational Fund** ⓘ *www.santamariadefe.org*, begun by English journalist Margaret Hebblethwaite (who still lives in the town), which sponsors education and craftwork (notably appliqué) and organizes local activities for visitors. From 1960 to 1976, Santa María de Fe was the home of the radically utopian **Ligas Agrarias Cristianas** (Christian Agrarian League) until suppressed by Stroessner. For those wishing to stay the night, there is a hotel on the plaza ($$, www.santamariahotel.org).

Santa Rosa

Returning to Ruta 1, 22 km east of San Ignacio Guazú at Km 248, is Santa Rosa (population 8902). Founded in 1698, only the Nuestra Señora de Loreto chapel of the original Jesuit church survived a fire. The current building dates from 1884. The chapel houses the **Museo Jesuítico de Santa Rosa** ⓘ *unhelpfully advertised as the Museo Oratorio de Nuestra Señora de Loreto, T0858-285221, www.portalguarani. com (under 'Museums and cultural centres'), daily but by appointment only 0730-1130 and 1430-1600, so ask at the parroquia first; free,* on the walls of which are frescoes in poor condition. Exhibits include four singular sculptures considered to be some of the greatest works of the Hispanic American Baroque: the *Annunciation*, the *Pietá*, the *Archangel Gabriel* and the *Virgin of Loreto*. Don't miss the Koki Ruiz sculpture of the mythological Kurupí, in the middle of Plaza Mariscal Estigarribia. The town can be reached by daily buses from San Ignacio Guazú.

San Patricio

Ruta 1 heads south from Santa Rosa to San Patricio (population 3607), at Km 252, which is important not as a destination in itself but as the starting point for two different trips. The first soon deviates from Ruta 1 to reach the towns of Santiago and Ayolas, which are accessed by taking a right turn at Cruze Isla Timbo 10 km out of San Patricio. **Santiago** is a further 18 km, and Ayolas, on the banks of the Río Paraná, is 34 km from Santiago.

The second possibility is to remain on Ruta 1 heading east for 56 km and then take a right turn onto Desvío a San Cosme y Damián for 25 km until reaching the town. San Cosme y Damián can also be reached from Ayolas by taking a recently paved road that follows the Río Paraná, although there are no service stations en route.

Santiago

At Km 262 on Ruta 1 a road leads first to the former Jesuit *reducción* at Santiago (population 7702) and then the town of Ayolas founded 1840 on the banks of the Río Paraná. Santiago was once an important Jesuit centre (founded 1651) and has a modern church containing a fine wooden carving of Santiago slaying the Saracens. There is more wooden statuary next door in the **Museo de Arte Jesuítico de Santiago** ⓘ *T975-762008, www.portalguarani.com (under 'Museums and cultural centres'), Mon-Sat 0800-1100, 1400-1700, Sun 0900-1100, free, guided tour US$2.15 (ask around the village for the key-holder).* There is an annual **Fiesta de la Tradición Misionera**, in January or February, with music, dance, horsemanship and other events.

Ayolas

Some 34 km beyond Santiago, Ayolas (population 15,386) is good for fishing and influenced by the construction of the Yacyretá dam built by **Entidad Binacional Yacyretá** (EBY). In the town is the **Museo Regional Yacyretá**. Some 12 km from Ayolas, the **Refugio Faunístico de Atinguy** ⓘ *http://www.portalguarani.com, Mon-Sat 0830-1130, 1330-1630; Sun and holidays 0830-1130, free*, is run as a research and educational facility to study the fauna affected by the dam. EBY also has a reserve on the **island of Yacyretá** itself (for visits to the project, T072-222141, or in Asunción T021-445055). To get there, cross the river to Ituzaingó, Argentina (linked via the road to Corrientes and Posadas).

San Cosme y Damián

San Cosme y Damián is the only ex-Jesuit mission in the country still used for religious services. When the Jesuits were expelled from Spanish colonies in 1767, the **church and ancillary buildings** ⓘ *Mon-Sat 0700-1130 and 1300-1700, US$5.50; T985-732956 for tickets, which are also valid for visits to La Santísima Trinidad de Paraná and Jesús de Tavarangue (see page 53)*, were unfinished. A huge restoration project has followed the original plans. Some of the *casas de indios* are in private use for other purposes, such as the cultural centre and parts of the **Centro de Interpretación Astronómica Buenaventura Suárez** ⓘ *T985-110047, daily 0700-2000; guide Rolando Barboza T985-732956*, which lies on the site of the original Jesuit observatory, the first built by Europeans in the New World. For the tourist committee contact T0985-110047; guide Rolando Barboza T0985-732956.

General Delgado to San Juan del Paraná

From San Patricio, it is 36 km to General Delgado (Km 288), and from there another 31 km to Coronel Bogado (Km 319), considered Paraguay's *chipá* (cheese bread with manioc) capital, and which functions as a major transportation depot as Rutas 1 and 8 connect here. Be sure to avail yourself of a bag or two; it's delicious and will last quite a long time without storage.

Carmen del Paraná Another 11 km brings you to Carmen del Paraná (Km 330, population 190), the rice capital of the country and situated on the northern bank of the Río Paraná, which has the new (2013) **Museo de Carmen del Paraná** ⓘ *Av Costanera, T0762-260415, www.portalguarani.com (under 'Museums and cultural centres'), daily 0800-1400, free*. Often mistakenly called the Museo Histórico Ferroviario – it is built as a replica of the town's former railway depot – the museum was largely funded by the nearby **Entidad Binacional Yacyretá** (www.eby.gov.py) and has fine displays of typical Guaraní costumes and daily life. The church is a 19th-century affair, but interesting for the three colonial-era indigenous-carved statues carried there by the Guaraní when they left the former *reducción* of Itapúa. Carmen del Paraná boasts a lovely riverside walkway, the Costanera, with three small sandy beaches fronting the Río Paraná. On the town's patronal feast day (16 June), there are plenty of regional games and music (many now extinct elsewhere) on display. Perhaps Carmen del Paraná's biggest claim to fame, however, is that many of its inhabitants are descendants of Czech, Slovak, Russian, Polish and Ukrainian immigrants who arrived after the First World War, as evidenced by much of the town's architecture, cuisine and educational and religious institutions.

San Juan del Paraná Another 35 km beyond Carmen del Paraná lies San Juan del Paraná (Km 365), which foreshadows what one can expect in Encarnación: shops, beaches and water sports geared to tourism, and the upmarket residential country club **Agua Vista** ⓘ *Av Fulgencio Yegros, T071-205400, www.aguavista. com.py,* which has the only USGA-certified golf course in Paraguay. It also hosts triathlons, bicycle races and regattas on the Río Paraná. Crossing the Mbói ka'e Bridge brings you to Encarnación.

Listings Jesuit missions

Where to stay

San Ignacio Guazú and around

$$ Hotel Rural San Ignacio Country Club
Ruta 1, Km 230, T0782-232895, gusjhave@hotmail.com.
With full board and Wi-Fi in cabins. Also has shaded camping, US$6 pp, without tent or meals, but other services included, hot water, electricity, tennis, swimming pool, ping-pong table, pool, impressive place and very helpful owner.

$$ Parador Altamirano
Ruta 1, Km 224, T0782-232334.
Modern, on outskirts, with a/c ($ pp without), recommended, 24-hr restaurant.

$$ Santa María Hotel
Santa María de Fé, T0781-283311/981-861553, www.santamariahotel.org.
With breakfast. Activities offered include day tours of Santa María and 2-week tours to other Jesuit towns and the region.

$$-$ La Casa de Loly
Mcal López 1595, San Ignacio, T0782-232362, http://lacasadeloli.com.py, on outskirts.

Nice atmosphere, cabañas and rooms, pool, a/c, with breakfast, other meals on request.

Santiago, Ayolas and San Cosme y Damián

$$ Hotel Nacional de Turismo Ayolas
Av Costanera, Villa Permanente, T072-222273, infohotelturismoayolaspy@ gmail.com.
Overlooking the river, popular with fishing groups.

Transport

San Ignacio Guazú and around
Bus Regular services to/from **Asunción**, US$4.50 *común,* up to 4½ hrs; to **Encarnación**, frequent, US$6 *común.*

Santa María de Fe
Bus From **San Ignacio** from the Esso station, 6 a day from 0500, 45 mins.

San Cosme y Damián
Bus From **Encarnación**, La Cosmeña and **Perla del Sur**, US$4, 2½ hrs.

At Km 370 on Ruta 1, the San Roque González de Santa Cruz bridge connects this busy port, the largest town in the region (founded 1615 as Itapúa, and known as 'La Perla del Sur'), with the Argentine town of Posadas across the Río Paraná.

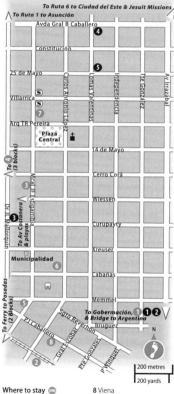

Encarnación

Where to stay 🛏
1 Casa de la Y
2 Central
3 Cristal
4 De La Costa
5 De La Trinidad
6 Germano
7 Paraná
8 Viena

Restaurants 🍴
1 América Grill
2 Brasiliani Grill & Pasta
3 Habib's
4 Heladería Mako
5 Hiroshima

The Encarnación of today is largely a modern city (population 94,572); the old town – or what remains of it above ground – has been badly neglected as it was due to be flooded when the Yacyretá-Apipé dam (the forerunner of the binational Yacyretá dam) was completed. Since the flooding, what is not under water has been abandoned and a modern town has been built higher up with a pronounced emphasis on catering to upmarket tourism... Paraguayan style. As a result, there are many new glitzy hotels, restaurants and cafés geared to travellers looking to spend time and money on upscale pursuits, and numerous tour agencies to cater to their interests. The city's restaurants, in particular, have gained a reputation for being every bit the equal or superior to those of Asunción. In fact, although the town exports large quantities of timber, soya, mate, tobacco, cotton and hides, tourism is increasingly the main economic driver.

In its rush toward economic prosperity, the town is fast losing its traditional, rural appearance, but its pre-Lenten **Carnival** is the best known in the country, rivalled only by that of Villarrica (which it exceeds in flashiness and revelry if not in traditional activities). If you're in town for the festivities, head to the Sambadromo Carnival on Avenida Costanera to purchase tickets (from US$11.50) in advance.

The mate ritual

Mate (pronounced *mattay*) is a bitter green tea made from the leaves of the yerba mate plant *(ilex paraguaiensis)* and is mildly stimulating, less so than caffeine, and effective at ridding the body of toxins as well as being mildly laxative and diuretic. It was encouraged by the Jesuits as an alternative to alcohol, and grown in their plantations.

The mate container is traditionally made from a hollowed gourd, but can be made of wood or tin. There are also ornate varieties made to traditional gaucho patterns by the best silversmiths.

Dried *yerba* leaves are placed in the mate to just over half full, and then the whole container is shaken upside down using a hand to prevent spillage. This makes sure that any excess powder is removed from the leaves before drinking. Hot water is added to create the infusion, which is then sipped through the *bombilla*, a perforated metal straw. One person in the group acts as *cebador*, trickling fresh hot water into the mate, having the first sip (which is the most bitter) and passing it to each person in turn to sip. The water must be at 80-82°C (just as the kettle starts to 'sing') and generally mate is drunk *amargo* – without sugar.

The town is a good base for visiting nearby Jesuit missions, the inland **Playa San José**, and the newly constructed **Avenida Costanera Pacu Cua** along the Río Paraná, the city's crown jewel and on which it has pinned much of its tourism hopes. A few blocks over, outside the bus terminal (C A López y Cabañas, T071-202412) there are yellow horse-drawn carriages called *karumbés*, which make for a pleasant way to see the city (US\$2.50 per person, free on weekends). Bizarrely, Encarnación, in the extreme south, holds the distinction of being the only place in Paraguay outside of the Chaco ever to receive snowfall.

Ruta 1 officially ends at the roundabout connecting it to Avenida Caballero, where Paraguay's Ruta 6 begins.

Border with Argentina

The San Roque road bridge connects Encarnación with Posadas. Formalities are conducted at respective ends of the bridge. Argentine side has different offices for locals and foreigners; Paraguay has one for both. The **Argentine Vice Consulate** is at Artigas 960, T071-201066, cenca@mrecic.gov.ar, Monday-Friday 0800-1300. **Brazilian Vice Consulate**, Memmel 452, T071-203950/206335950 (see Facebook). There are moneychangers at the Paraguayan side of the bridge but it's best to change money in town. **Note** Paraguay is one hour behind Argentina, except during Paraguayan summer time (October-April).

Santísima Trinidad del Paraná and Jesús de Tavarangue

Although not along Ruta 1, and most easily accessed from Encarnación along Ruta 6 towards Ciudad del Este, the two best-preserved Jesuit former *reducciones* in Paraguay are Santísima Trinidad del Paraná (33 km from Encarnación) and Jesús de Tavarangue (12 km from Santísima Trinidad, turning left at the service station after leaving town). These are both recognized as UNESCO World Cultural Heritage Sites (whc.unesco.org/en/list/648).

Santísima Trinidad del Paraná The hilltop site of **Trinidad** ⓘ *T985-810053 (parroquia), www.turismojesusytrinidad.com.py, US$5.50, Oct-May 0700-1900, Apr-Sep 0700-1730, light and sound show Thu-Sun 2000 in summer, 1900 in winter; guides T985-772803 or T985-753997; joint ticket gives access to Jesús and San Cosme y Damián*, built 1706-1760, has undergone significant restoration. Note the partially restored church, the carved stone pulpit, font and other masonry and relief sculpture. Also partially rebuilt is the bell tower near the original church (great views from the top). You can also see another church, a college, workshops and indigenous living quarters. It was founded in 1706 by Padre Juan de Anaya; the architect was Juan Bautista Prímoli. For information or tours (in Spanish and German), ask at the visitor centre. There are three *artesanías* nearby and craft demonstrations in the afternoon. The **Jesuito Snack Bar** at the turn-off from the main road has decent food.

One kilometre from Trinidad is **Parque Ecológico Ita Cajón** ⓘ *T985-726971, US$3.50*, an enormous clearing where the stone was quarried for the former *reducción*. Frequent folklore events are held here. The **municipal tourist office** ⓘ *T071-270165, Mon-Fri 0700-1300*, in the centre of town also has information.

Jesús de Tavarangue About 12 km northwest of Trinidad, along a rough road (which turns off 300 m north from Trinidad entrance) is **Jesús de Tavarangue** ⓘ *T985-734340, www.turismojesusytrinidad.com.py, Oct-May 0700-1900, Apr-Sep 0700-1730, US$5.50 as above, guides available*, now a small town where another group of Jesuits settled in 1763. In the less than four years before they were expelled they embarked on a huge construction programme that included the church, sacristy, *residencia* and baptistry, on one side of which is a square tower. There is a fine front façade with three great arched portals in a Moorish style. The ruins have been restored. There are beautiful views from the main tower. The **municipal tourist office** ⓘ *T071-270150, Mon-Fri 0700-1300*, in the centre of Jesús also has information and a brochure.

German colonies on the road to Ciudad del Este

From Trinidad on Ruta 6, the road goes through or near a number of German colonies including **Hohenau** (7.5 km from Trinidad, Km 36 as measured by Ruta 6 markers). Less than 1 km before it, **Parque Manantial** ⓘ *500 m from the main road, T0775-232250, www.encarnacion.com.py/guia-comercial/parque-manantial, Tue-Sun 0090-2000, US$2.50, pool US$3.50, camping US$4.75*, is in a beautiful location and has three pools, a good restaurant, bar and lovely camping ground with complete facilities. Activities include horse riding, tours of the countryside by jeep and cross-country tours to the nearby Jesuit ruins. It's a good place to stop off on the way to Ciudad del Este. Major credit cards are accepted and national phone calls can be made at no extra charge.

The next colony is **Obligado**, 2 km from Hohenau (turn left 2 km after the HGA printing plant); it has an ATM in the centre of town. About 6 km further north is **Bella Vista**, at Km 42 (bear right at the roundabout topped by a giant yerba mate gourd), which also has ATM. As the roundabout indicates, Bella Vista is considered the yerba mate capital of Paraguay. From the port at the southern end of Avenida Mcal Samaniego you can cross the Río Paraná to Corpus in Argentina by ferry (car ferry on weekdays only; foot passengers US$2.50), making a good circuit between the Paraguayan and Argentine Jesuit missions. There are immigration and customs facilities. For information on Bella Vista, see www.bellavista.gov.py.

There are several yerba mate plantations in the region, two of which are among the country's largest producers: **Pajarito** ⓘ *Av Mcal Samaniego y Corpus, T0767-240240, www.pajarito.com.py*, and **Selecta** ⓘ *Av Mcal Samaniego Km 4.5, T0767-240247, www.selecta.com.py*; they accept visitors with advance notice.

Tourist information

There are tourist offices on the **Costanera**, *Av Costanera, Padre Bolik y RN1, T071-202989, www.encarnacion.com. py, daily 0700-1900*.
San Roque bridge, *daily 0700-1900*.
Trinidad, *T0985-753997*, Mon-Fri 0700-1500.

Where to stay

Encarnación

$$$-$$ De La Costa
Av Rodríguez de Francia 1240 con Cerro Corá, T071-205694, www.delacostahotel.com.py.
Smart hotel on the new Costanera, with pool, garden, parking and restaurant.

$$$-$$ De La Trinidad
Estigarribia y Memmel, T071-208099, www.hoteldelatrinidad.com.py.

New tower-block hotel of a good standard, close to bus station, 6 categories of room with all modern facilities, with spa, restaurant, pool, parking.

$$ Cristal
Estigarribia 1157 y Cerro Corá, T071-202371, www.hotelcristal.com.py.
City hotel with pool and restaurant, helpful staff.

$$-$ Casa de la Y
Carmen de Lara Castro 422, entre Yegros y Molas, Barrio San Roque, T985-77 8198, http://casadelay.wix.com/casa-de-la-y.
Quiet location a short distance from most attractions and facilities (bus terminal transfer US$5), 1 double room, 1 dorm with bath, garden, breakfast included, other meals available, Wi-Fi, welcoming and attractive.

$ Central
Mcal López 542 y C A López,
Zona Baja, T071-203454,
soyparte@encarnacion.com.py.
With breakfast, nice patio,
German spoken.

$ Germano
General Cabañas y C A López, opposite
bus terminal, T071-203346.
Cheaper without bath or a/c, German
and Japanese spoken, small, very
accommodating. Highly recommended.

$ Paraná
Estigarribia 1414 y Tomas R Pereira y
Villarrica, T071-204440.
Good breakfast, helpful. Recommended.

$ Viena
PJ Caballero 568, T071-205981.
With breakfast, German-run,
good food, garage.

**German colonies on the road to
Ciuidad del Este**

$$$ Papillón
Ruta 6, Km 45, Bella Vista, T0767-240235,
www.papillon.com.py.
A/c, pool, gardens, very pleasant,
German, French, English, Flemish
spoken, excellent and popular
restaurant, full and half-board available.
Highly recommended. Organizes
excursions in the area.

Restaurants

Encarnación

$$$-$$ Brasiliani Grill & Pasta
Just before Aduana checkpoint heading
to Puente Internacional, T071-202181.
Brazilian buffet and pizzas in a new
restaurant that is already very popular.

$$ América Grill
Ruta Internacional y Av San Blas,
T071-204829.
Good *churrasquería*.

$$ Hiroshima
25 de Mayo y L Valentinas (no sign), T071-
203505. Tue-Sun 1130-1400, 1900-2330.
Excellent Japanese, wide variety,
fresh sushi.

$ Habib's
Mallorquín y Curupayty.
Of the many restaurants now serving
Arabic, Lebanese and Turkish food in
Encarnación, this is one of the best at
a great price. Excellent Middle Eastern
fast food, especially a regional favourite,
lomito árabe.

$ Heladería Mako
Av Caballero 590 y Lomas Valentinas,
T202116, www.makos.com.py.
Ice cream, cakes, coffee and more.
A huge hit in the high season.

Transport

Bus The bus terminal is at Mcal
Estigarribia y Memmel. Good
cheap snacks. To/from **Asunción**,
8 companies including **La Encarnacena**
(recommended, T071-203448, www.
laencarnacena. com.py), **Rysa** (T071-
203311), at least 4 a day each, 6 hrs,
US$10.50-12. Stopping (*común*) buses
are much slower (6-7 hrs), US$6.75.
To **Ciudad del Este**, US$11, several
daily, 4 hrs.

Border with Argentina
Bus Take any 'Posadas/Argentina'
bus from opposite bus terminal over
the bridge, US$1.25, 30 mins. Keep all
luggage with you and retain bus ticket;
buses do not wait. After formalities

(queues common), use ticket on next bus.

Cycles are not allowed to use the bridge, but officials may give cyclists a lift.

Ferry costs US$2. Immigration formalities must be undertaken at the main offices.

Taxi costs US$12.50 (at least).

Santísima Trinidad del Paraná and Jesús de Tavarangüé

Bus Many go from **Encarnación** to and through Trinidad, take any bus from the terminal marked Hohenau or Ciudad del Este, US$2.50 (beware overcharging).

A **taxi** tour from Encarnación costs about US$40. Bus direct **Encarnación–Jesús** 0800; buses run **Jesús–Trinidad** every hr (30 mins, US$1), from where it is easy to get back to Encarnación, so do Jesús first. Last bus Jesús–Trinidad 1700; also collective taxis, return Trinidad–Jesús US$6. No buses on Sun. Enquire locally as taxis may overcharge

East of Asunción: Ruta 2

To the east of the Río Paraguay lie the most fertile lands and the most populated region of the country. Of the vast rainforests that once covered it, only a few isolated patches have not been converted to farmland. Fortunately, a few remnants of the once enormous Atlantic forest, such as the San Rafael National Forest, have been turned into protected areas. Rutas 2, 3 and 7 (a continuation of Ruta 2) all head east towards the border with Brazil, taking the traveller near tranquil villages known for their arts and crafts, German colonies, the occasional Franciscan mission, and small towns associated with the country's deceptively bellicose past.

Unlike Ruta 1, Paraguay's Ruta 2 begins in Asunción itself, at the intersection of Avenida Sivio Petrossi y Brasil in Barrio San Roque. It winds its way through the nondescript suburbs of Fernando de la Mora (Km 6) and San Lorenzo (Km 10, where it intersects with Ruta 1) before reaching Capiata (Km 19). From here the vistas improve dramatically.

Best for
Atlantic forest ▪ German colonies ▪ Small towns

At Km 30 on Ruta 2, Itauguá (population 148,721) was founded in 1728 and is now Paraguay's fastest-growing city. The old town lies two blocks from the main highway.

It is famous for its *ñandutí* or spiderweb lace of which there are some 320 different designs. Prices are lower than in Asunción and the quality is better; there are many makers. Almost all of the best workshops are located directly off the highway and can be accessed by bus. To watch the lace being made, ask around.

Worth seeing are the **market** ① *Mon-Sat 0800-1130, 1500-1800, closed Sun*, the church of **Virgen del Rosario**, the **Museo de Historia Indígena** ① *Km 25, daily 0800-1130, 1500-1800, US$0.75*, a beautiful collection of carvings of Guaraní mythological creatures, and the **Museo Parroquial San Rafael** ① *daily 0800-1130, 1500-1800, free*, with a display of indigenous art and Franciscan artefacts.

There is a four-day **Festival de Ñandutí** in early July, including processions and the crowning of Señorita Ñandutí. Many of Paraguay's best traditional musicians perform during the festival and this is the time to visit if looking for spectacular examples of the multicoloured lace. There are also musical evenings on **Viernes Culturales** (Cultural Fridays) in January and February.

Itauguá is the birthplace of Juan Crisóstomo Centurión, the only Paraguayan military leader to win a battle in the War of the Triple Alliance and an architect of the country's rebirth. For information on Itaguá see www.itaugua.com.py. There are frequent bus connections with Asunción (one hour, US$0.75).

At **Capiatá** (Ruta 2, Km 20, fine colonial church), a left turn leads to Areguá (population 15,814), Paraguay's strawberry capital and a centre of quality crafts, ceramics in particular.

Founded in 1541, this is a pretty colonial village, 30 km east of Asunción and also easily reached from Luque's main road. It sits on the slopes above **Lago Ypacaraí**. From Asunción, take the bus from Shopping del Sol, Nos 11 or 111. It may take scenic route through villages, 45-60 minutes (may take longer if traffic is heavy); alternatively take local bus to Capiatá and change.

Formerly the summer capital of the country's elite, from its attractive church at the highest point in town there is one of the best views of the lake, its two nearby *cerros* (Kõi and Ita'o) and surroundings.

It has an interesting ceramics cooperative, a museum, arts and crafts exhibition and, on its outskirts, a remarkable **Dominican convent** ① *T0291-433500, daily 0800-1700, US$2.25*, originally a castle built for Francisco Solano López and his mistress Eliza Lynch, and later purchased by one of Paraguay's grandes dames, **Carlota Palmerola**. Guided tours of the convent and other sites in town leave

Sundays at 0900 and return at 1500, from Senatur's office in Asunción (T021-433500, US$6.50).

There is also a memorial in the centre to its most famous son, Gabriel Casaccia Bibolini, who many consider to be the founder of modern Paraguayan literature. There is a good German-run restaurant in the centre of the village. From here boat trips run across the lake at weekends to San Bernardino.

★San Bernardino and Lago Ypacaraí
upmarket city bolthole; tranquil off season

San Bernardino
At Km 48 on Ruta 2 a branch road, 8 km long, leads to San Bernardino (population 7720), originally a Swiss-German colony settled by the eminent botanist Emilio Hassler and known locally as 'Samber', on the east bank of Lago Ypacaraí. In the past few decades it has replaced Areguá as the country's summer resort for the rich. The lake, 24 km by 5 km, has facilities for swimming and water sports and sandy beaches (ask locally about pollution levels in the water). There are frequent cruises from the pier during the tourist season. It is now the main vacation spot for much of Asunción from December to February, which means that it is lively and crowded at weekends in the summer, with concerts, pubs and nightclubs, and has become rather commercialized. During the week and off season it is a tranquil resort town, with lakeside tourism clearly the main draw. It's not possible to swim in the lake but there are boat tours.

In the town itself, **Casa Büttner** ⓘ *Colonos Alemanes, T984-933158, free*, is worth a visit. An estate built by the German immigrant Julio Büttner in 1882, it saw Paraguay's first automobile and bus, and was also the site of the country's first formal carpentry and ice-making factories. The house is still owned by Büttner's descendants, and part of it serves as the town's library, a tea house and a crafts centre. It also has a wealth of information for travellers.

Boats can be hired and there is good walking in the neighbourhood, for example, from San Bernardino to **Altos**, which has one of the most spectacular views of the lake, wooded hills and valleys (round trip three hours). Several more costly activities normally not associated with Paraguay (eg waterskiing and paragliding) are also available in town. Shortly after the turn-off from the main road towards San Bernardino is a sign to **La Gruta**; turn right here to a secluded park, Ypacaraí. There are grottos with still water and overhanging cliffs. No buses run after 2000 and taxis are expensive.

The town is one of these few in Paraguay to have an official tourist guide agency **SanBer Tour** ⓘ *T981-607829, sanber_tour_py@hotmail.com*, which offers five different tours. For the actively inclined, **Aventura Xtrema** ⓘ *NS de la Asunción y Hassler, T961-682243, www.aventuraxtrema.com.py*, specializes in extreme outdoor trekking in the area. The **tourist office** ⓘ *Casa Hassler, between General Morinigo and Emilio Hassler, T0512-232974, http://sanbernardino.gov.py/casa-hassler*, is also the town's cultural centre.

ON THE ROAD

National parks and nature tourism

This abundance of wildlife, particularly birds, is most visible in the Chaco, especially in its remote national parks, along the Río Pilcomayo, and the frontier with Bolivia. It is been estimated that the Pantanal has the highest concentration of fauna in the New World. Current estimates include between 10,000 and 13,000 plant species, 100,000 invertebrates (including 765 species of butterfly), 300 species of fish, 120 reptiles, 100 amphibians, 687 birds and 171 mammals. For more details, visit **Fauna Paraguay** (www.faunaparaguay.com). Paraguay has an extensive network of state-protected areas, 94 in all, covering almost 7% of the country's territory. Some fall within three biosphere reserves, Chaco Paraguayo, Bosque Mbaracayú and Río Apa. Exactly what constitutes a protected area is confusing and the criteria can change frequently. To complicate matters further, of this number, 38 are private reserves which are maintained by outside entities (in some cases, the Itaipú and Yacyretá dam authorities) but which are in one way or another supervised by Paraguay's **Secretaría Nacional de Turismo** (Senatur, www.senatur.gov.py) or **Secretaría del Ambiente** (SEAM, www.seam.gov.py). Many of these protected areas exist solely on paper, and the whole system is under-funded. As beautiful and unique as these areas are, infrastructure is in most cases rudimentary at best (if it exists at all), and visiting them is not always easy. Always contact the relevant institutions and authorities first, and never venture in without prior permission

Lago Ypacaraí

Returning to Ruta 2, at Km 37 you'll reach the town of Ypacaraí. A little more than 1 km after this, the first of Ruta 2's *cabinas de peaje* (toll booths) appears. (The other is in Coronel Oviedo at Km 125.) There isn't much to see in town unless you're there when the **Festival del Lago de Ypacaraí** is held (a week in August or September), in which case there are a number of lakeside events, some here and others in neighbouring San Bernardino. The festival is now quite popular, and has folklore, handicrafts, dance, art and theatre awards.

Listings San Bernardino and Lago Ypacaraí

Where to stay

Other than those listed, there are plenty of hotels, many with good restaurants, from the super luxury **Sol de San Ber** down. Book hotels in advance during fiestas.

$$$ Del Lago
Tte Weiler 401 y Mcal López,
near lake in town, T0512-232201,
www.hoteldellago.org.
With breakfast, attractive 1888 building renovated as a museum, upgraded, safe, regional decor, restaurant, bar and grill, pool, lovely gardens.

(and a good all-terrain vehicle). The most reliable online source is the National Parks of Paraguay blog (http://nationalparksofparaguay.blogspot.com). A 2014 map of SEAM's Sistema Nacional de Areas Protegidas del Paraguay (SINASIP) can be found on its Calendario 2015, available on its website.

For the reserves managed by the Itaipú and Yacyretá authorities, contact the relevant environmental departments. For private reserves contact the following conservation NGOs: **Guyra Paraguay** (Gaetano Martino 215 y Tte Ross, Asunción, T021-223567, www.guyra.org.py) which has a wealth of information as well as the expertise to organize tailor-made ecotours to all parts of the country, including some of the more remote locations (highly recommended); **Fundación Moisés Bertoni para la Conservación de la Naturaleza** (Prócer Carlos Argüello 208, Asunción, T021-608740, www.mbertoni.org.py) which manages the Mbaracayú Reserve, one of two remaining pristine Atlantic forest reserves in the region, as well as the lesser-known Tapyta Reserve; **Pro Cosara** (Hohenau II, Itapúa, T0768-295046, http://procosara.org) which works for the protection of the San Rafael Nature Reserve in eastern Paraguay and which welcomes volunteers at the ecological station (www.faunaparaguay.com/ecosaravolunteers.html); **Para la Tierra** (San Pedro del Ycuamandiyú, T0985-260074, www.paralatierra.org) which works for the protection of the Laguna Blanca Reserve and also welcomes volunteers. **Desarrollo Turístico Paraguayo** (DTP, offices in Asunción, Encarnación and Ciudad del Este, www.dtp.com.py), the country's largest and best-known tourism agency, can organize adventure tours to different parts of the country.

$$$ Pueblo Hotel San Bernardino
C 8 entre C 5 y Mbocayá, T0512-232195,
pueblohotel@gmail.com.
Swimming pool, a/c, by the lake.
Weekend packages also available.

$$ Los Alpes
Ruta General Morínigo Km
46.5, 3 km from town, T0512-
232083, www.hotellosalpes.com.py.
Lovely gardens, 2 swimming pools, excellent self-service restaurant, children's playground, beach 1 km away, frequent buses to centre.

Camping

Brisas del Mediterráneo
Ruta Kennedy a 2000 m
from Copaco, T0512-232459,
www.paraguay-hostel.com.

With campsite (US$10.50, Oct-Apr), rooms ($$-$), meals, beach and games.

What to do

Aventura Xtrema, *NS de la Asunción y Hassler, T981-682243, San Bernardino, www.aventuraxtrema.com.py.* Offers backpacker tours and a variety of adventure tours: horse riding, caving, canoes, hiking, cycling and more.

Transport

Bus From **Asunción**, 3 companies: **Altos**, **Loma Grande** and **Ciudad de San Bernadino**, every 10 mins, 45 km, 1-2 hrs, US$1.25.

quiet town with a huge basilica and immense annual festival

Caacupé (population 30,738) is a popular resort and religious centre on the Azcurra escarpment. The centre is dominated by the modern cathedral, **Our Lady of the Miracles** ⓘ *entry free but small fee to climb the tower*, with a copper roof, stained glass and polychrome stone esplanade. It is the largest church in the country (and one of only 14 cathedrals) and was consecrated by Pope John Paul II in 1988. There is an ATM on the plaza between the supermarket and **Hotel El Mirador**.

Hundreds of thousands of people – estimates run to more than 5% of the country's entire population – from Paraguay, Brazil and Argentina flock to the shrine, especially for the **Fiesta de la Inmaculada Concepción** on 8 December, known locally as the Fiesta de la Virgen de Caacupé, or the 'Black Virgin'. Besides fireworks and candlelit processions, pilgrims watch the agile gyrations of Paraguayan bottle-dancers; they weave in intricate patterns while balancing bottles in pyramid formation on their heads. The top bottle carries a spray of flowers and the more expert dancers never drop a single petal. The bottles contain blessed water, which is believed to come from the nearby spring of Tupasy Ykuá, which the Virgin revealed to early settlers. Caacupé is also well known for its Carnival celebrations.

Tobatí

Tobatí, a town 15 km north of Caacupé along a marked branch road (Carretera Pedro Juan Caballero), specializes in woodwork. The town's highly regarded Villa Artesenal is 1-km walk from the bus stop outside the house of the late **Zenon Páez**, a world-famous sculptor. It produces wonderful masks (some reputedly of pre-Columbian ancestry), coca-fibre hammocks and furniture. The villa also has a small permanent exhibit and annual traditional handicrafts fair. There are some amazing rock formations on the way to Tobatí. To get there, take a bus from the corner below the park on the main Asunción road in Caacupé.

Listings Caacupé

Where to stay

Cheaper than Lago Ypacaraí. Prices increase during the Fiesta de la Inmaculada Concepción.

$$-$ Katy María
Eligio Ayala y Dr Pino, T0511-242860, beside Basílica, www.katymaria.com.
Well-kept, welcoming, Wi-Fi.

$ El Mirador
T0511-242652, on plaza.
With bath.

$ Virgen Serrana
Plaza, T0511-242366.
A/c, cheaper with fan.

Tourism farm

$$$$ Estancia Aventura
Km 61.5, Ruta 2, T981-441804, www. estancia-aventura.com.

91 ha of countryside, 7-day packages. Owner speaks German, English, Spanish. Good, horse riding, tennis, swimming, tours, can arrange airport pick-up from Asunción. Expensive but worth it.

Transport

Bus From **Asunción**, US$1.25, get off at Basilica (closer to centre) rather than Caacupé station.

Piribebuy

remote town with an important wartime history

Beyond Caacupé, at Km 71 on Ruta 2, a paved road (Ruta Paraguarí–Piribebuy) runs 13 km due south to the town of Piribebuy, founded in 1636 and noted for its strong local drink, *caña*. In the central plaza is the church (1640), with fine sculptures, high altar and pulpit. Piribebuy (population 13,106) is officially one of Paraguay's 'heroic cities' in recognition of its staunch defence during a major battle in the War of the Triple Alliance (1869), commemorated by the **Museo Histórico Comandante Pedro Pablo Caballero** ⓘ *Mariscal Estigarribia y Yegros, T976-380355, http://museopedrocaballero.wordpress.com, Mon-Fri 0700-1700, Sat and Sun 0700-1130, free*, which also contains pristine artefacts from the Chaco War. This event ranks with the Battle of Acosta Ñu in the country's history as an example of the Paraguayans fierce resistance in the face of almost unbelievable odds. It was here that an untrained battalion composed mostly of children, outnumbered almost 20 to one and led by a school master, fought against and prevented the advance of Brazilian troops. There are buses from Asunción with **Transportes Piribebuy**.

Around Piribebuy

Near the town are the attractive falls of Piraretá and more than 15 hot springs (popular at weekends). The Ruta Paraguarí–Piribebuy continues via Chololó, 13 km south, and reaches Ruta 1 at Paraguarí, 28 km from Piribebuy (see page 41).

Between Pirbebuy and Paraguarí is an outdoor and adventure centre, **Eco Reserva Mbatoví** ⓘ *T021-444844 from Asunción, or T971-659820, for reservations and information visit www.mbatovi.com.py, US$35*, with a visitor centre. It includes an outdoor pursuits course and a three-hour guided walk, taking in early settlements, local folklore and beautiful scenery. For further information on Mbatoví, see page 41.

Listings Piribebuy

Where to stay

$$$ La Quinta
10 km from Piribebuy, 19 km from Paraguarí, 82.5 km from Asunción along Ruta 1 and then branch road from Piribebuy (take bus to Piribebuy then bus to Chololó, bus passes in front of hotel),
T971-117444, www.laquinta.com.py.
Price for 4 sharing in cabins, also suites, also open for day visits, own stream and is close to falls at Piraretá and Chololó.

$ Viejo Rincón
Maestro Fermín López y Tte Horacio Gini, T0515-212251.
A reasonable choice.

Returning to Ruta 2, a turn-off just before entering Eusebio Ayala (Km 71) onto the Ruta Ciudad Eusebio Ayala–Caraguatay goes 22 km to Caraguatay, 4 km from which is the Vapor Cué National Park, where boats from the War of the Triple Alliance are preserved.

For those interested in the history behind these unusual boats, most of which were constructed in Britain or by British naval engineers, see www.histarmar.com.ar/armadasextranjeras/paraguay/vaporcue-1.htm. Although officially a national park, it is more of an open-air museum. Next to the (indoor) museum is a hotel with pool, **Hotel Nacional de Vapor Cué** ($$, T0517-222395). Frequent buses run from Asunción to Caraguatay, from where local ones can be caught to the park's entrance.

Caraguatay

Some 20 km northeast of Eusebio Ayala on a branch road from Ruta 2 lies Caraguatay (population 13,965), a singular town with an interesting history. Founded by the Spanish in 1770, it later served as the summer residence of Francisco Solano López and his Irish mistress Eliza Lynch. The town's centre boasts several beautiful colonial-era buildings and, on 24 September, it celebrates the feast day of its patron saint, the **Virgen de las Mercedes**, with traditional dances and music that are no longer seen elsewhere in the country.

Remarkably for a town of less than 5000 inhabitants, it has given the country three presidents. Caraguatay is also the recipient of an interesting international economic consequence: it sends more workers abroad than any other municipality in Paraguay, and the remittances returned have made it one of the country's more upscale communities, with amenities and public services not easily found elsewhere. Many expatriate Paraguayan workers spend decades overseas, sending most of their earnings back home where the funds are first used to build solid houses for immediate and extended family members, with additional funds collectively allocated to community improvement projects. In several cases, the workers never see these improvements until they return for good to retire in the town. Paraguay's best-known leader of the 20th century (apart from the infamous dictator Alfredo Stroessner), José Félix Estigarribia – for whom it seems there is a street named in every town in the country – was born in Caraguatay. For more information, see http://caraguatay-ciudad.blogspot.com.

Coronel Oviedo and around
a couple of excellent wildlife reserves well worth a detour

Leaving Eusibio Ayala and following Ruta 2, the road through the small communities of **Itacurubí de la Cordillera** (Km 86) and **San José de los Arroyos** (Km 102) before reaching Coronel Oviedo (population 64,486) at Km 132. There is a toll booth just before the entrance to the town. Located at the junction of west–east highway Ruta 2 and the major north–south Ruta 8, it is an important transport centre, although hardly worth a stop unless you are fortunate enough to catch the highly acclaimed **Orquesta Filarmónica Ovetense** when in town. Buses drop passengers for connections at the junction (El Cruce), and from here connections are made to Villarrica along Ruta 8 and Ciudad del Este along Ruta 7.

Ruta 7 to Ciudad del Este
For the vast majority of travellers, paved Ruta 7, which runs 195 km through farmed areas and woods and across the Caaguazú Hills, is the route taken. From Coronel Oviedo it continues in a nearly straight line to the spectacular 500-m single-span 'Friendship Bridge' across the Paraná at Ciudad del Este, from which Foz do Iguaçu (Brazil) – the ultimate destination for many – is reached.

Ruta 8 to Villarrica
Ruta 8, perpendicular to Ruta 7, runs north for 60 km to Santa Rosa del Mbutuy, then another 32 km to Cruce Tacuara on the outskirts of San Estanislao, where it bears right and continues 197 km as Ruta 3 all the way to Yby Yaú in the north.

At **Santa Rosa de Mbutuy** (Km 56, parador, restaurant, petrol station), 100 km north of Coronel Oviedo on Ruta 8, and some 36 km before Cruce Tacuara, Ruta 3 meets Ruta 10. From here Ruta 10 branches off northeast, heading to the Brazilian frontier on the Río Paraná at Salto de Guaíra, some 259 km distant, named after the waterfalls now under the Itaipú lake. There is a rarely seen but wonderful 900-ha wildlife reserve, **Refugio Biológico Binacional Mbaracayú** ⓘ *www.itaipu.gov. br/es/sala-de-prensa/noticia/areas-silvestres-protegidas-de-itaipu*, administered by the Itaipú complex (some 80 hellish kilometres northwest from Hernandarias). This route is about 317 km from Coronel Oviedo and is the most direct.

Salto de Guaíra
Salto de Guaíra, a free port in the upper reaches of the Río Paraná which trades heavily with neighbouring Brazil, can also be reached via Ruta 7 travelling eastward from Coronel Oviedo to the outskirts of Ciudad del Este (192 km) and then by a paved highway (the Supercarretera Itaipú) which passes through the neighbouring city of Hernandarias, north through Nueva Esperanza and on to where it meets Ruta 10 at Cruce Carolina Andrea. This route is roughly 415 km from Coronel Oviedo and takes much longer, but affords vistas of Paraguay rarely seen by visitors. For information, see www.saltodelguaira.net.

Reserva de la Biosfera del Bosque Mbaracayú
To visit, first contact the Fundación Moisés Bertoni in Asunción for details (see National parks, page 60 for address); US$7.50. 2 bus companies from Asunción to Curuguaty, daily, 6 hrs, US$20. From Curuguaty to Villa Ygatimí local buses take 1 hr, not all paved, so if driving a 4WD vehicle is a must. From Villa Ygatimí it is 25 km to the park on a dirt road, T034-720147 for the park staff to arrange transport; US$15, 3-5 hrs.

Not to be confused with the nearby Refugio Biológico Binacional Mbaracayú established by Itaipú (see above), this federally protected reserve, shortlisted for inscription in UNESCO's list of World Heritage Sites, covers 64,406 ha of Paraguay's rapidly disappearing interior Atlantic forest. It is one of the country's few protected areas that is well managed (albeit by a foundation, not the government), and is the largest area representative of this ecosystem in good conservation status in Paraguay. The importance of its biodiversity cannot be overstated: the relatively small area contains 53% of all mammal species (nearly 100) and 58% of all bird species (411) found in eastern Paraguay. There are trails (US$2 with guide; US$5 to hire bike, guide US$6 extra), canoes (US$8, guide US$8), waterfalls (US$20) and spectacular viewpoints. There are also two indigenous communities, the Aché and Guaraní.

The visitor centre is a 3-km walk from the entrance, and there's a small museum at **Villa Ygatimí** (one of the oldest towns in the country, founded in 1539). Lodging can also be found here (Jejui-Mi T034-720147, 13 rooms, each with Wi-Fi and air-conditioning, with or without bath, and meals are available). Packages of seven, 15 and 30 days can be booked. Run by **Fundación Moisés Bertoni**, members of the Aché tribe assemble on its grounds at daybreak.

Listings Coronel Oviedo and around

Where to stay

Coronel Oviedo and around

$$-$ Quincho Porá
Aquidaban 235, Coronel Oviedo,
T0521-202963/972-86 4236,
www.2cv-tours.de/hostel.htm.
Owned by Walter Schäffer who runs Citröen 2CV and Land Rover tours in Paraguay and South America. Good hostel, German/Paraguayan, lots of information, hammock space, bar.

Reserva de la Biosfera del Mbaracayú

$$ Jejuí-Mi
near entrance to reserve, T034-720147.
Administered by Fundación Moisés Bertoni. Meals US$8. Aché indigenous community occasionally gathers on grounds at sunrise.

Transport

Salto de Guaíra
Bus **Asunción** to **Coronel Oviedo**, US$4. From Asunción to **Saltos del Guaíra**, US$10.50-12, 4 companies, several daily; to **Ciudad del Este**, US$12. **To Brazil** Regular launches cross the lake to Guaíra, 20 mins. Also hourly bus service, 30 mins, US$1.75. Buses run north of the lake to Mondo Novo, where they connect with Brazilian services. Brazilian consulate is at Canindeyú 980, casi Pasajae Morán, T046-242305.

Villarrica (population 56,385), 43 km south of Coronel Oviedo on Ruta 8, is delightfully set on a hill rich with orange trees. Founded in 1570, thanks to slave traders raising the area from Brazil, it was moved seven times – thus earning its nickname 'Wandering City' – before settling in its current location in 1682.

It is a very pleasant, friendly place, with a fine cathedral built in traditional style with veranda, and various pleasant parks. The **Museo Municipal Maestro Fermín López** ① *Natalicio Talavera y Juan Pablo II, T0541-41521, www.villarrik.com/2012/03/ museo-fermin-lopez.html, Mon-Fri 0715-1900, Sat 0800-1200, closed Sun, free,* behind the church in a wonderfully restored building dating from the War of the Triple Alliance has a foreign coin collection; please contribute. In the centre, there are many historic older buildings (tours available), in particular, the **Club Porvenir Guaireño** ① *Beato Roque González y Coronel Félix Bogado, www.rotaryvillarrica. org,* and the **Palacete Municipal y Teatro** ① *C A López y Mcal F S López, www. villarrik.com/2012/03/teatro-municipal.html.* Both should be seen for a glimpse of Paraguay's faded early 20th-century architectural glory. The nearby **Parque Ortiz Guerrero** on Dr Bottrel y Azara is a pleasant spot to take in the sights and relax. Products of the region are tobacco, cotton, sugar, yerba mate, hides, meat and wine produced by German settlers.

There is a large student population and the town is the cultural hub of the region and second only to Asunción in terms of literary output and academic reputation. Its **Carnaval Guaireño** is one of the most spectacular events in the nation (outdone – and not by much – only by Encarnación's) and attracts bigger and bigger crowds every year. For more information see www.villarrica.gov.py, or www. villarricacheciudad.com. There is an ATM at gas station at northern end of town.

Swiss-German colonies

There are several Swiss-German colonies near Villarrica. Some 7 km north on Ruta 8 is an unsigned turn-off to the east in front of the Patio-Pepe Gästehaus, then 20 km to tiny **Colonia Independencia**, which has some beautiful beaches on the river (popular in summer). Colonia Independencia is also the access point for the hotly contested Ybytyruzu Reserve 21 km out of town, which offers some of Paraguay's most beautiful scenery from **Cerro Akati**. Unfortunately, the reserve receives no protection from the government, has been encroached on by loggers and landless groups, and is forced to depend entirely on volunteer efforts. As a result, its future as a reserve is in doubt. The trek to the *cerro* is arduous but rewarding. See www.salvemoslos.com.py/rrmy.htm for information.

German-speaking travellers can also visit the German cooperative farms (these are not Mennonite communities, but rather German settlements established in the early 20th century). It's a great mate- and wine-producing area and, at harvest time, there is a wine festival. There is also a good beer festival in October.

Where to stay

Villarrica
Book rooms in advance during fiestas.

$$$ Villarrica Palace Hotel
*Ruta 8 Blas Garay, turn right on road
entering Villarrica, T0541-42832,
www.sosahoteles.com/villaricapalace.*
Large modern hotel, restaurant, parking,
pool, sauna.

$$ Ybytyruzú
*C A López y Dr Bottrell, T0541-42390,
www.hotelybytyruzu.com.*
Best in town, breakfast, more with
a/c, restaurant.

$ Guairá
Mcal López y Talavera, T0541-42369.
With bath and a/c, cheaper with
fan, welcoming.

Colonia Independencia

$$ Hotel Tilinski
Out of town, T0548-265240.
Peaceful, German spoken, swimming
pool (filled with river water), meals
for residents.

Swiss-German colonies

$$ Hotel Tilinski
*Near Colonia Independencia,
T0548-265240, www.hotel-tilinski.com.*
Peaceful, German spoken, swimming
pool (filled with river water), meals
for residents.

Restaurants

Villarrica
Many eating places on CA López and
General Díaz. At night on the plaza with
the Municipalidad stands sell tasty,
cheap steaks.

Transport

Villarrica
Bus To **Coronel Oviedo**, US$2.50. To
Asunción, frequent, US$4.50-6, 3½ hrs
(La Guaireña). Also direct service to
Ciudad del Este, see below.

Colonia Independencia
Bus Direct to **Asunción**, 3 daily (US$5,
4 hrs), as well as to **Villarrica**.

Villarrica also serves as an ideal access to the San Rafael National Forest.

To reach the park, one of the few that is relatively easy to access from a main road, take Ruta 8 south 26 km until just south of Numí and then bear left onto a branch road. From here it's another 85 km, passing through the only town of note, **San Juan Nepomuceno**, at about the halfway point. Here you take a right turn onto yet another branch road (marked with sign for park) and travel another 72 km on a dirt road until reaching the park's northern entrance. **Note** Some guidebooks mistakenly suggest reaching the park from either Coronel Bogado or Encarnación; both of these options take far longer and the route is more difficult.

San Rafael is noted for two things: its pristine Atlantic forest – one of the last on the continent – and its bird population (close to 450 different species have been recorded). The park, as with so many in Paraguay, relies heavily upon outside caretakers. One of the most important of these is **Procosara** ① *Hohenau II in Itapúa, T0768-295046, http://procosara.org*, which runs a reserve in the park and also offers tours, volunteering opportunities and cabins for rent in **Estancia Nueva Gambach** at the southern tip of the reserve.

Ciudad del Este & the Río Paraná

From Asunción, Ciudad del Este is a 332-km straight shot across Rutas 2 and 7. The city is a chaotic crossroads for all manner of merchandise (much of it illegal, including the world's largest stolen car market), while the giant Itaipú dam has irreversibly changed the landscape.

Further north along the river lies the remote Pantanal, home to more species of aquatic life than anywhere else on the continent.

Best for
Duty-free shopping ▪ Enormous dam ▪ Waterfalls

Originally founded as Ciudad Presidente Stroessner in 1957 and 327 km from Asunción at the eastern terminus of Ruta 7, this was the fastest-growing city in the country until the completion of the Itaipú hydroelectric project, for which it is the centre of operations. Ciudad del Este (population 396,091), Paraguay's second-largest city, has been described as the biggest shopping centre in Latin America, attracting Brazilian and Argentine visitors looking for cheap electrical goods, watches and perfumes.

Like Encarnación, Ciudad del Este has a large expatriate Middle Eastern and Asian population, is situated along the banks of the Río Paraná and is a gateway to other destinations in the region. The comparisons end there, however. The city is also a counterfeiter's paradise and can be quite dangerous. Check everything properly before making a purchase and ensure that shops pack what you actually bought. The main shopping street, Avenida San Blas, is lined with shopping malls and market stalls, selling a huge variety of goods. Almost any vehicle advertised for sale, should you be tempted, was stolen in Brazil or Bolivia. Many jewels and stones are also counterfeit; be especially careful with touts advertising amethysts or emeralds. Watch the exchange rates if you're a short-term visitor, or fancy a whirl at one of the city's 10 casinos. No-one would ever call Ciudad del Este a cultural draw, but it does have the interesting **Museo El Mensú** ⓘ *Av Gral Bernardino Caballero next to the Municipalidad, Mon-Fri 0800-1700, free*, with exhibits on what the area that now makes up the city looked like many years ago. Parts of the city are dirty and frantic during business hours, but away from Avenida San Blas and Avenida Adrián Jara the pace of life is more relaxed and the streets and parks are green and quiet.

Waterfalls around Ciudad del Este
The **Monday Falls (Saltos del Monday)** ⓘ *Ruta Saltos del Monday, T061-552512, www.itaipu.gov.py/en/tourism/monday-river-waterfalls, daily 0730-1700, US$1*, where the Río Monday drops 80 m into the Río Paraná gorge, are well worth seeing. A return taxi from Ciudad del Este costs US$25. Located just 10 km south in the adjacent town of Presidente Franco in the **Saltos del Río Monday Municipal Park** ⓘ *http://rutajesuitica.com.py/en/alto-parana/saltos-del-rio-Monday, camping possible (US$1), meals available*, and accessed along the ruta (marked) by the same name, these are Paraguay's largest waterfalls and were proclaimed a protected area by the government in 2012. Trails among the vegetation lead visitors to belvederes and walkways from which they are able to view the river's 45-m gorge. For those looking for adventure, steep rocky walls are ideal for rappelling, trekking and mountain climbing right on the edge of the powerful flowing waters. Try to arrive before dusk when thousands of swallows perform aerial acrobatics around the falls before settling in for the night.

Presidente Franco and around

Some 27 km south of the city via Avenida Monday and then the Acceso Parque Moisés Bertoni, at the southernmost edge of Presidente Franco, is **Parque Nacional Moisés Bertoni**, although it is more easily reached by boat. The park began as a nationally recognized monument to the Swiss diplomat (and later the Paraguayan minister of agriculture) Moisés Bertoni, whose 199-ha summer retreat (greatly reduced from its original size) is kept as a museum of sorts.

Bertoni, a much loved figure in Paraguay's cultural, political, scientific and social history, and one of the few prominent individuals in his day to actively support the rights of indigenous peoples, was later honoured as the namesake for the vitally important ecological organization, the **Fundación Moisés Bertoni** (www. mbertoni.org.py). The eclectic house-laboratory encloses a **Scientific Museum** ⓘ *T05561-599 8040, http://rutajesuitica.com.py/es/alto-parana/museo-cientifico-moises-bertoni, Tue-Sun 0730-1500, free*, with more than 7000 volumes amassed by Bertoni. For access by boat, contact DTP (T061-511779) or **Mavani Tour Operator** (T061-514386).

Ciudad del Este

Also in Presidente Franco, just across the river from the municipal park, are the little-known private **Maharishi Reserves** I and II, 6 km out of town on 343- and 77-ha properties very close to the Saltos de Monday. There are interpretive trails and nature walks, ideal for less mobile visitors and children. See www.hernandarias. com/not_praver.php?id_praver=99 for information (in Spanish).

North of Ciudad del Este is the popular beach resort and biological refuge, **Tatí Yupí** ⓘ *T061-599 8473, www.itaipu.gov.py/en/tourism/tati-yupi-sanctuary*.

Border with Brazil

The border crossing over the Friendship Bridge to Foz do Iguaçu on the Brazilian side is very informal, but is jammed with vehicles and pedestrians all day long. It is also the only land crossing between the two cities, and marks the eastern termination of Paraguay's Ruta 7 and the western one for Brazil's Ruta 277.

200 metres
200 yards

Where to stay ●
1 Austria
2 California
3 El Caribeño
4 Convair
5 Mi Abuela
6 Munich

Restaurants ●
1 Cantina Napoli, Patussi Grill, Pizza Hut, Relax Heladería y Café
2 Gouranga
3 Yrupé

From Paraguay, on buses from Asunción to Foz do Iguaçu and beyond, non-Paraguayans get out at Aduana Paraguaya for an exit stamp, then the bus takes all passengers across the river to Aduana Brasil–Paraguai on the other side for the entry stamp. Note that buses marked 'Foz do Iguaçu' do not – in spite of both the law and what you may be told – always stop at Aduana Paraguaya before crossing into Brazil; and after 2000, they never do. This is not likely to cause problems with Brazilian authorities, but make absolutely certain to pick up a Brazilian exit stamp before returning to Paraguay – otherwise you may have some explaining to do upon returning to Ciudad del Este. The problem is common though and you aren't likely to have any worries as long as your paperwork is in order. The rule of thumb for all border crossings between Paraguay and Brazil, Bolivia and Argentina is the same: make sure you get all entry and exit stamps. For local bus services, see Transport, page 75.

If you are arriving in Paraguay from Brazil, crossing by bus (from 0500 until 1930 every 10-15 minutes) is recommended. No passport stamps are required to visit Ciudad del Este for the day, assuming you are returning to Brazil within 24 hours. Motorcycle taxis (helmet provided, hang on tight) are a good option if you have no luggage. There are lots of minibuses, too. On international buses, eg from Florianópolis to Ciudad del Este and Asunción, or from Foz do Iguaçu to Asunción, the procedure is as follows: non-Brazilians get out at Aduana Brasil–Paraguai for an exit stamp, then take the bus across the bridge to Aduana Paraguaya where everyone gets out for an entry stamp.

Take note that although Ciudad del Este is a tax-free shopping destination for Brazilians, the same is not true in reverse. Technically there is a Paraguayan import tax of up to 60% on anything purchased in Brazil costing more than US$300. This applies to Paraguayan citizens only (and even then is not usually enforced), but keep all receipts for any items purchased in Brazil and make sure the price is denominated in reais. There are local banks (open Monday-Friday 0730-1100) in town and many *casas de cambio* on Adrián Jara y Curupayty. There is a friendly tourist office in the customs building on the Paraguayan side, open 24 hours. You can get out of the bus here, rather than going to the bus terminal. Taxis wait just beyond immigration, US$4.50-5.50 to most places in Ciudad del Este, but settle the price before getting in as there are reports of exorbitant fares. Remember to adjust your watch to local time (Brazil is one hour ahead). Although Paraguay observes DST (Daylight Saving Time) throughout the country, only some states in Brazil (including Paraná) do. **Brazilian Consulate** ① *Ciudad del Este, Pampliega 205 y Pa'í Pérez, T061-500984, http://deleste.itamaraty.gov.br, Mon-Fri 0800-1400, issues visas.*

Tip...

There is a *casa de cambio* 20 m beyond the entry post; rates are no different from in town and much safer than using the street changers, of which there are plenty. Money changers (not recommended) operate at the bus terminal.

Border with Argentina

Crossing from Paraguay to Argentina (Puerto Iguazú) is not done directly from Ciudad del Este. (In fact, the nearest bridge with direct access to Argentina from Paraguay is hundreds of kilometres to the southwest in Encarnación.) Instead, the procedure is similar to crossing to Brazil. You cross the Friendship Bridge, and at immigration catch a bus marked 'Puerto Iguazú' (US$1.50). You don't need a Brazilian visa, but you will need an entry stamp once you cross into Argentina (obtained at Aduana Iguazú-Control de Frontera, just after crossing the other Friendship Bridge between Brazil and Argentina). The bridge connects directly to Argetina's Ruta 12, which parallels the Río Paraná as far as Resistencia before turning south to Buenos Aires. If you plan to return to Paraguay the same way, you'll need an exit stamp from Argentine immigration. **Argentine Consulate** ① *Av Boquerón y Adrián Jara, Edificio China p 7, T061-500945, www.embajada-argentina. org.py/V2/consulados/consulado-gral-en-cde, Mon-Fri 0800-1300.*

Listings Ciudad del Este *map p72*

Tourist information

Ciudad del Este tourist office
Adrián Jara y Mcal Estigarribia, by the urban bus terminal, T061-511626, 0700-1900, is helpful.
For information on Ciudad del Este, also see http://vivecde.com.

Where to stay

$$$ California
C A López 180, T061-501838, www.hotelcalifornia.com.py.
Several blocks from commercial area, large, modern with swimming pool, lit clay tennis court, attractive gardens, good restaurant.

$$ Austria
E R Fernández 165, T061-504213, www.hotelaustriarestaurante.com.
Above good restaurant, good breakfast, Austrian family, good views from upper floors, popular with shopping trips and groups. Warmly recommended.

$$ Convair
Adrián Jara y Pioneros del Este, T061-508555, www.hotelconvair.com.
In shopping district, comfortable, restaurant good, pasta festival on Thu, pool.

$$ El Caribeño
Fernández 136, T061-512460, http://hotelcaribeno.com.py.
On 3 floors around central car parking area, plain rooms but spotless, helpful. Recommended.

$$ Mi Abuela
Adrián Jara y Pioneros del Este, T061-500333, www.miabuelahotel.com.
Small, off a central patio, restaurant, opposite **Convair**.

$$ Munich
Fernández 71 y Miranda, T061-500347.
A/c, frigobar, parking. Recommended.

Restaurants

$$ Patussi Grill
*Monseñor Francisco Cedzchiz casi
Av Alejo García, T061-502293,
www.patussigrill.com. Tue-Sat 1100-
1500, 1800-2300, Sun 1100-1600.*
Good *churrasquería*, Wi-Fi. At the same
junction, T061-513204, is **$$ Cantina
Napoli**, pizzas and pastas. Also **Pizza
Hut**, **Relax Heladería y Café**, T061-
501671, Mon-Fri 1600-2400, Sat 1630-
0100 (closed Sun) and **Librería El Foro**.

$ Gouranga
Pampliega y Eusebio Ayala, T061-510362.
Vegetarian restaurant with a menu
that changes daily, also juices, desserts,
sandwiches, burgers, etc.

$ Yrupé
*Curupayty y A Jara (part of Executive
Hotel, T061-512215, www.executivehotel.
com.py/restaurant.html), T061-509946.*
Good buffet lunch for US$5.50 including
ice cream. Also desserts, coffee
and Wi-Fi.

Shopping

Supermarkets
Area Iris (A Jara y Av Pioneros del Este.
Open 0700-1930, Sun 0800-1300). Serves
good value meals. **Shopping del Este**
(by Puente de Amistad), has good
restaurants. Another good collection of
restaurants is at **Centro Gastronómico
Epoca** (on Rogelio Benítez), some
distance southeast of centre, near Lago
de la República. Other shopping centres,
eg **Corazón**, have a Patio de Comidas.

Transport

Ciudad del Este
Air International airport, Aeropuerto
Guaraní; departure tax US$16. To
Asunción, **TAM** daily en route from
São Paulo. **TAM**, Av San Blas con
Patricio Colman, Km 2, Shopping Zuni,
T061-506030-35.

Bus Terminal is south of the centre,
T061-510421 (No 4 bus from centre,
US$0.70, taxi US$5, recommended).
Many buses to and from **Asunción**,
US$13-16 *rápido*, 4½ hrs, at night only;
US$12 *común*, 5 hrs minimum. **Nuestra
Señora** recommended (they also have
an office in Shopping Mirage, Pampliega
y Adrián Jara), **Rysa** (T061-510396) and
others. To **Villarrica**, many daily with
La Guaireña and **La Carapagueña**, US$7,
4 hrs. To **Pedro Juan Caballero**, 7 hrs,
overnight US$15, **García** and others.
To **Concepción**, **García**, 11 hrs, 2 per
day. To **Encarnación** (for Posadas and
Argentina), paved road, frequent, 4-5 hrs,
US$10 (this is cheaper than via Foz do
Iguaçu). There are international services
to Argentina and Brazil.

Border with Brazil
Bus 2 bus companies cross the
international bridge between Ciudad
del Este and Foz's bus terminals: **Pluma**,
T061-510434, www.pluma. com.br, daily
0700-1830 each way every 10 mins,
30-40 mins, US$2, and **Rafagnin**,
T+55-45-3523 1986 (Brazil; no office in
Paraguay) 0800-1900, US$3; speak to the
driver about waiting at the immigration
posts at either end of the bridge. Most
buses will not wait at immigration, so
disembark to get your exit stamp, walk
across the bridge (10 mins) and obtain
your entry stamp; keep your ticket and
continue to Foz on the next bus free.

Paraguayan taxis cross freely to Brazil (US$30), but it is cheaper and easier to walk across the bridge and then take a taxi, bargain hard. You can pay in either currency (and often in Argentine pesos). Obtain all necessary exit and entry stamps.

Border with Argentina

Direct buses to **Puerto Iguazú**, leave frequently from outside the terminal, US$2.50. If continuing into Argentina, you need to get Argentine and Paraguayan stamps (not Brazilian), but bus usually does not stop, so ask driver if he will. Also check what stamps you need, if any, if making a day visit to Puerto Iguazú.

★Itaipú and around

the world's second largest dam; controversial but fascinating

Close to Ciudad del Este, Itaipú is a huge hydroelectric project covering an area of 1350 sq km and still subject to controversy among environmental groups (it completely inundated the former Parque Nacional Sete Quedas and has led to numerous floods; peaceful protests continue on an almost daily basis there as well as near the plant itself).

Currently the world's second-largest generator of renewable clean energy, the project is well worth a visit. It is staggering to comprehend the enormity of Itaipú: almost all of Paraguay's electricity is generated by it, along with some 20% of Brazil's, the world's fifth-largest country! If you don't have much time, the **Panoramic Tour** is your best bet. Starting from the central belvedere, visitors have a 360-degree view of the power plant featuring the dam and spillway. Visits are made on Itaipú buses (for visitors traveling on their own) or on tourist buses, for those on organized tours. A documentary on Itaipú is shown prior to the departure. The tour lasts approximately 1½ hours and is available on both sides of the border. In Brazil, visitors can also choose to take the **Combined Power Plant/Eco-museum Tour**, or the **Combined Power Plant/Biological Sanctuary Tour**, a 2-km walk along an eco-trail inside the Bella Vista Sanctuary (see below). Tours start hourly 0800-1600, US$8. (Note that certain sections of the tour may be restricted to over 14-years-olds.) For general information, T061-599804, www.itaipu.gov.py, daily 0800-1800.

Bella Vista ⓘ www.itaipu.gov.py/en/turismo/biological-sanctuary, is an interesting biological sanctuary, which has successfully re-settled flora and fauna dislodged during the construction of the dam. Guided tours lasting 2½-hours take place Wednesday to Monday (0830, 1000, 1430, 1530, US$6).

There is a **light show** every Friday and Saturday, 1830-2100, US$4.75 (very popular so book in advance, T061-599804, or call the Brazilian side, T+55 45 3520-6676, www.itaipu.gov.py/en/tourism/lighting-of-the-dam). Free bus tours of the external facilities run daily and include a film show (several languages). Take your passport as the dam is a federal installation and straddles Paraguay and Brazil.

Buses going to Hernandarias will drop you at the Centro de Recepción de Visitas on Avenida Tancredo Neves.

Around Itaipú

On the way to Itaipú is **Zoológico Regional y Vivero Forestal** ① *on the Supercarretera Itaipú, 11.5 km from Ciudad del Este, T061-599 8632, www.itaipu. gov.py, guided visits on the hour Tue-Sun 0800-1100, 1400-1600, free,* with a zoo and nursery containing native animals and plants. The nursery has more than 500 species and annually plants some 200,000 ornamental, forest and fruit trees. Nearby is the **Museo de la Tierra Guaraní** ① *Supercarretera Itaipú, T061-599863, www.itaipu.gov.py/en/tourism/museum-guarani-land, Tue-Sun 0800-1700, free*, which offers a view of the science and culture of the Guaraníes via natural history displays and interactive screens.

Hernandarias and around

① *Frequent services from Ciudad del Este to Hernandarias, US$1.* This rapidly growing city just north of Ciudad del Este really took off with the building of the Itaipú complex. There isn't a great deal to see in the city itself, as it is essentially a town grown up around a shipping terminal. However, for those wishing to avoid the chaotic mess that Ciudad del Este can be, Hernandarias (population 86,213) is a quieter alternative, and one that has most of what you'd need to purchase or rent if striking out on your own to explore the upper Paraná region. Both the Itaipú International Airport and the entirety of the Paraguayan side of the Itaipú hydroelectric complex are located here. For information, see www.hernandarias. com. There are frequent buses from Ciudad del Este (US$1).

From Hernandarias, the **Supercarretera Itaipú** runs north for 158 km, passes through Nueva Esperanza (the only town of any size) and on to Cruce Carolina Andrea, where it meets Ruta 10 and turns right for Salto de Guaíra (see page 65). This road also provides access to two biological sanctuaries on Lago Itaipú, **Itabó** (at 15,208 ha and 80 km from Hernandarias) and, a further 80 km north, **Limoy**, with 14,828 ha. Prior permission to visit is required from **Flora y Fauna Itaipú Binacional** ① *12 de Junio, Ciudad del Este, T061-598040, daily 0730-1300 and 1400-1700.* For information on both reserves, which one day will be connected by an ecological sub-corridor, see www.itaipu.gov.py/es/medio-ambiente/reservas-y-refugios. At present, camping is not allowed in either of the reserves.

Iguazú Falls
(Foz do Iguaçu)

Along the border (and shared with Brazil and Argentina), the Iguazú Falls are the top draw for most visitors coming to Paraguay, with tourism numbers now eclipsing even the Jesuit missions and the charms of Asunción.

The mighty falls are the most overwhelmingly magnificent in all of South America. So impressive are they that Eleanor Roosevelt remarked "poor Niagara" on witnessing them (they are four times wider). In 2012 they were confirmed as one of the New Seven Wonders of the Modern World. Viewed from below, the tumbling water is extraordinarily beautiful in its setting of begonias, orchids, ferns and palms. Toucans, flocks of parrots, cacique birds and great dusky swifts dodge in and out along with myriad butterflies (of which there are at least 500 different species). Above the impact of the water on basalt rock, hovers a perpetual 30-m-high cloud of mist in which the sun creates blazing rainbows.

Best for
Butterflies ▪ Hiking ▪ Mighty falls ▪ Mist

Essential Iguazú Falls (Foz do Iguaçu)

Finding your feet

To visit the Falls from Paraguay is pretty straightforward. You cross the bridge from Ciudad del Este to Foz do Iguaçu by bus, motorcycle-taxi or on foot (see page 72 and Transport, page 75). Go to the Terminal Urbana in Foz and catch a bus to the Brazilian national park. To continue to the Argentine side take a bus (it's too far to walk) from the Terminal Urbana to Puerto Iguazú and catch another bus to the Argentine national park. There are also direct buses between Ciudad del Este and Puerto Iguazú, which do not stop in Brazil (see page 74 and Transport, page 76) from where regular buses run to the park. At all border posts make sure you get the correct stamps for your visit, especially if staying overnight in Brazil or Argentina. If you need a visa for either country, make sure you have got one. For border crossings, see pages 72, 74, 82 and 83.

Getting around

On the Brazilian side, a bus service runs from the entrance to the park every 10 minutes in both directions, connecting the falls with the park administration and other activities. On the Argentine side of the park, a small train runs every 30 minutes from the visitor centre to the beginning of

Tip...

See www.cataratasdoiguacu.com.br for information about the Brazilian side of the falls, and www.iguazuargentina.com for the Argentine side.

Tip...

From October to March (daylight saving dates change each year) Brazil is one hour ahead of Paraguay.

the trail to the Garganta del Diablo. Transport between the Brazilian and Argentine parks is via the Ponte Tancredo Neves as there is no crossing at the falls themselves.

Time required

To visit both sides and return to Paraguay in a day by public transport would be very difficult. It's worth spending a day on each side of the falls, especially if you want to enjoy walking some of the trails or take a boat trip.

Visiting the Iguazú Falls

On both sides of the falls there are national parks (see pages 80 and 88 for prices and visitor information). Both countries offer a different perspective. While the majority of the falls are in Argentina, the Brazilian park offers a superb panoramic view of the whole falls and is best visited in the morning when the light is better for photography. The Argentine park offers closer views of the individual falls in their forest setting with its wildlife, though to appreciate these properly you need to go early and get well away from the main visitor areas. Both parks have visitor centres, and tourist facilities on both sides are constantly being improved, including for the disabled.

The Ponte de la Amistad links Ciudad del Este with Foz do Iguaçu. There is little in the way of formalities at the border if you are not stopping in Brazil. It is still a fair distance to the falls: too far to walk. There are memorable views from the Brazilian visitor centre.

Parque Nacional Foz do Iguaçu

T045-3521 4400, www.cataratasdoiguacu.com.br. The park is open daily 0900-1700. Tickets cost US$17 payable in reais, Argentine pesos, euros, dollars or credit card, or online by credit card, includes obligatory transport within the park (discounts for Mercosur, Brazilian and local residents). From the Terminal de Transporte Urbano in Foz do Iguaçu, take a bus or taxi to the visitor centre at the park's entrance, Km 21 from Foz (40 mins). From the entrance, shuttle buses leave every 10-15 mins, stopping first at Park Administration.

1 Around the falls

➡ Iguazú Falls
1 Around Iguazú Falls, page 80
2 Foz do Iguaçu, page 83
3 Puerto Iguazú, page 89

Where to stay 🛏
1 Camping e Pousada Internacional
2 Hostel Inn Iguazú
4 Hostel Natura & Paudimar Campestre
5 Hotel Das Cataratas
6 Posada 21 Oranges
7 Pousada Evelina
8 Sheraton Internacional Iguazú Resort
9 Pousada Cataratas

The Brazilian national park was founded in 1939 and the area was designated a World Heritage Site by UNESCO in 1986. Fauna most frequently encountered are little and red brocket deer, South American coati, white-eared opossum, and a subspecies of the brown capuchin monkey. The endangered tegu lizard is common. Over 100 species of butterfly have been identified, among them the electric blue morpho, the poisonous red and black heliconius and species of *Papilionidae* and *Pieridae*. The birdlife is rewarding for birdwatchers. Five members of the toucan family can be seen.

At the park entrance is a smart **visitor centre**, with toilets, ATMs, a small café, a large souvenir shop and a Banco Itaú *câmbio* (1000-1500). An **Exposição Ecológica** has information about the natural history of the falls and surrounding park (included in entry fee; English texts poor). Nature lovers are advised to visit first thing in the morning or late in the afternoon, preferably in low season, as crowds can significantly detract from the experience of the falls and surrounding park (at peak times, like Semana Santa, up to 10,000 visitors arrive every day).

Next is the start of the **Poço Preto Trail** (9 km through the forest to the river,

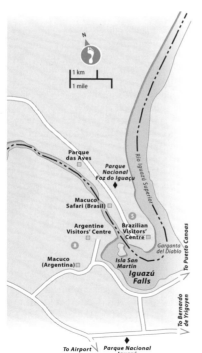

walking or by bicycle), then the **Bananeiras Trail** and **Macuco Safari** (see page 87). After 10 km the bus stops at the start of the **Cascadas Trail** and the **Hotel das Cataratas**, and finally at the end of the road, **Porta Canoas**. There are Portuguese, Spanish and English announcements of the five stops.

The 1.5-km paved **Cascadas Trail** is an easy walk, taking you high above the Rio Iguaçu, giving splendid views of all the falls on the Argentine side from a series of galleries. At the end of the path, you can walk down to a boardwalk at the foot of the Floriano Falls which goes almost to the middle of the river to give a good view of and a light spraying from the Garganta del Diablo. There is also a viewing point almost under the powerful Floriano Falls, a dramatic view. From here, 150 steps lead up to the Porto Canoas complex (there is a lift for those who find stairs difficult); you can also return the way you came, and walk a little further along the road.

The **Porto Canoas** complex consists of a big souvenir shop, toilets, a smart buffet restaurant, a café and *lanchonete*, all with good view of the river above the falls. Return to the visitor centr by the free shuttle bus. The whole visit will take around two hours, plus time for lunch. Never feed wild animals and keep your distance when taking photos; coatis have been known to attack visitors with food.

Foz do Iguaçu and around

Now a modern city, 28 km from the falls, Foz (population 263,508) has a wide range of accommodation. The bird zoo, **Parque das Aves** ① *Rodovia das Cataratas Km 16, 100 m before the entrance to the falls, T045-3529 8282, www. parquedasaves.com.br, 0800-1730, US$12*, has received frequent good reports. It contains Brazilian and foreign birds, many species of parrot and beautiful toucans in huge aviaries through which you can walk, with the birds flying and hopping around you. There are other birds in cages and a butterfly and hummingbird house.

Tip...

There are good communications by air and road with the main cities of southern Brazil, plus frequent cross-border links to Argentina and Paraguay, see Transport, page 87.

On the Río Paraná 12 km north, the **Itaipu dam** ① *short bus tours, US$8.75, or full tours including the interior of the dam, US$22, and night views, Fri-Sat 2000, US$5; children and seniors half price for all visits, check times with tourist office, T0800-645 4645, www.itaipu.gov.br, www.turismoitaipu.com.br*, is the site of the second-largest power station in the world, built jointly by Brazil and Paraguay (see page 76). Take your passport and wear long trousers and sensible shoes if you're going on the tour; the best light for photography is in the morning. Construction of this massive scheme began in 1975 and it became operational in 1984. Several beaches can be visited around the lake. A large reforestation project is underway and six biological refuges have been created on the lakeshore in both countries. There is also the **Ecomuseu de Itaipu** ① *Av Tancredo Neves, Km 11, T0800-645 4645, www.itaipu.gov.br/en/tourism/eco-museum, Tue-Sun 0830-1630, US$3.25*, and **Refúgio Biológico Bela Vista** ① *www.itaipu.gov.br/en/turismo/biological-sanctuary, closed Tue, 4 visits a day from the visitor centre, US$6.50*, an animal rescue centre and home to the fauna displaced by the dam, both geared to educate about the preservation of the local culture and environment (that part which isn't underwater). Recommended. In addition there is the **Polo Astronômico** ① *T045-576 7203, Tues-Sun at 1000 and 1600, Fri-Sat also 1830 (1930 in summer), US$6.50*, a planetarium and astronomical observatory.

Border with Argentina

All foreigners must get exit and entry stamps both in Brazil and Argentina every time they cross the border, even if it is only for the day. It is your responsibility to get the stamps. If riding a taxi make sure it stops at both border posts, if riding a city bus, ask for a transfer, get off at the Brazilian border post and get on the next bus through without paying again. If entering Brazil, be sure you also get the entry card stamped. **Argentine consulate** in Foz ① *Travessa Eduardo Bianchi 26, T045-3574 2969, Mon-Fri 1000-1500*.

Between October and February Brazil is one hour ahead of Argentina. It takes about two hours to get from Foz to the Argentine falls; very tiring when the weather is hot.

Border with Paraguay

The Ponte de Amizade/Puente de la Amistad (Friendship Bridge) over the Río Paraná, 6 km north of Foz, leads straight into the heart of Ciudad del Este. Paraguayan and Brazilian immigration formalities are dealt with at opposite ends of the bridge. Ask for relevant stamps if you need them. The area is intensively patrolled for contraband and stolen cars; ensure that all documentation is in order. Brazil is one hour ahead of Paraguay. **Paraguayan consulate** in Foz ① *R Marechal Deodoro 901, T045-3523 2768, Mon-Fri 0900-1700.*

➡ **Iguazú Falls**
1 Around Iguazú Falls, page 80
2 Foz do Iguaçu, page 83
3 Puerto Iguazú, page 89

2 Foz do Iguaçu

Where to stay		Restaurants	Bars & clubs
1 Arterial	7 Foz Presidente II	1 Atos	9 Armazém
2 Baviera	8 Luz	2 Bier Garten	10 Capitão Bar
3 Best Western Tarobá	9 Pousada da Laura	3 Búfalo Branco	11 Oba! Oba!
4 Del Rey	10 Pousada El Shaddai	5 Marias e Maria	12 Pizza Park Bar
5 Foz Plaza	11 Pousada Evelina	6 Oficina do Sorvete	
6 Foz Presidente I	12 San Juan Tour	7 Rafain	
		8 Zaragoza	

Tourist information

Secretaria Municipal de Turismo
Av das Cataratas 2330 (midway between town and the turn-off to Ponte Tancredo Neves), T045-2105 8100, 0700-2300, www.pmfi.pr.gov.br.
Very helpful, English spoken.

Airport tourist office (open 0800-2200), is also good, gives map and bus information, English spoken. Helpful office, free map, at the **rodoviária** (daily 0700-1800), English spoken. Also at the **Terminal de Transporte Urbano** (daily 0730-1800). Tourist information

Where to stay

Check hotel websites for internet prices and special offers. Av Juscelino Kubitschek and the streets south of it, towards the river, are unsafe at night. Many prostitutes around R Rebouças and Almirante Barroso. Taxis are only good value for short distances when you are carrying all your luggage.

$$$ Best Western Tarobá
R Tarobá 1048, T0300-210 2727, www.hoteltaroba.com.br.
Bright and welcoming, small pool, nice rooms, helpful, good breakfast (extra), good value. Recommended.

$$$ Foz Presidente I and II
(I) R Xavier da Silva 1000 and (II) R Mcal Floriano Peixoto 1851, T045-3572 4450, www.fozpresidentehoteis.com.br.
Good value, decent rooms, restaurant, pool, Number 1 is convenient for buses.

$$$ San Juan Tour
R Marechal Deodoro 1349, T045-2105 9200, www.sanjuanhoteis.com.br.
Cheaper if booked online. Comfortable, excellent buffet breakfast, popular, good value. Recommended. The more expensive **San Juan Eco** is on the road to the falls.

$$$-$$ Baviera
Av Jorge Schimmelpfeng 697, T045-3523 5995, www.hotelbavieraiguassu.com.br.
Chalet-style exterior, on main road, central for bars and restaurants, comfortable.

$$$-$$ Del Rey
R Tarobá 1020, T045-2105 7500, www.hoteldelreyfoz.com.br.
Nothing fancy, but perennially popular, little pool, great breakfasts. Recommended.

$$$-$$ Foz Plaza
R Marechal Deodoro 1819, T045-3521 5500, www.fozplazahotel.com.br.
Serene and very nice, restaurant, pool. Also has a new annex.

$$$-$$ Luz
Av Gustavo Dobrandino da Silva 145, near rodoviária, T045-4053 9434, www.luzhotel.com.br.
Offers lots of packages, tours and promotional offers. Buffet restaurant, pool. Recommended.

$$ Pousada Cataratas
R Parigot de Sousa 180, T045-3523 7841, www.pousadacataratas.com.br.
Well-maintained modern rooms with decent hot showers, small pool, good value with regular discounts and promotions through the website.

Can organize tours and transfers to and from the airport and *rodoviária*.

$$ Pousada da Laura
R Naipi 671, T045-3572 3374,
Facebook: PousadaDaLaura.
$ pp in shared dorm with good breakfast. Secure, kitchen, laundry facilities, a popular place to meet other travellers.

$$-$ Arterial
Av José Maria de Brito 2661, T045-3573 1859, hotelarterial@hotmail.com.
Near *rodoviária*. Good value, huge breakfast, opposite is a 24-hr buffet restaurant.

$$-$ Pousada El Shaddai
R Rebouças 306, near Terminal Urbana, T045-3025 4490, http://pousadaelshaddai.com.br.
Fully equipped rooms, use of kitchen, English and Spanish spoken, pool.

$$-$ Pousada Evelina
R Irlan Kalichewski 171, Vila Yolanda, T045-3029 9277, http://pousadaevelinafoz.com.br.
Lots of tourist information, English, French, Italian, Polish and Spanish spoken, good breakfast and location, near Muffato Supermarket, near Av Cataratas on the way to the falls. Warmly recommended.

Camping

Camping e Pousada Internacional
R Manêncio Martins 21, 1.5 km from town, T045-3529 8183, www.campinginternacional.com.br.
For vehicles and tents, half price with International Camping Card, also basic cabins ($), helpful staff, English, German and Spanish spoken, pool, restaurant.

Note Camping is not permitted by the Hotel das Cataratas and falls.

Outside Foz do Iguaçu

$$$$ Hotel das Cataratas
Directly overlooking the falls, Km 32 from Foz, T045-2102 7000, www.belmond. com/hotel-das-cataratas-iguassu-falls.
Generally recommended, caters for lots of groups, attractive colonial-style building with pleasant gardens (where wildlife can be seen at night and early morning) and pool. Non-residents can eat here, midday and evening buffets; also à la carte dishes and dinner with show. An environmental fee of about US$10 is added to the room rate.

On the road to the falls (Rodovia das Cataratas) are several expensive modern hotels with good facilities (eg **Bristol Viale Cataratas**, www.vialecataratas. com.br, **Carimã**, www.hotelcarima.com. br, **San Martin**, www.hotelsanmartin. com.br), but for budget travellers, check out:

$$-$ Paudimar Campestre
Av das Cataratas Km 12.5, Remanso Grande, near airport, T045-3529 6061, www.paudimar.com.br.
In high season HI members only. From airport or town take Parque Nacional bus (0525-0040) and get out at Remanso Grande bus stop, by **Hotel San Juan Eco**, then take the free *alimentador* shuttle (0700-1900) to the hostel, or 1.2-km walk from main road. Camping as well (US$8), pool, soccer pitch, quiet, kitchen and communal meals, breakfast. Highly recommended. Tours run to either side of the falls (good value). **Paudimar** desk at *rodoviária*.

$ Hostel Natura
Rodovia das Cataratas Km 12.5, Remanso Grande, T045-3529 6949, www. hostelnatura.com (near the Paudimar).
Rustic hostel with a small pool set in

fields. Rooms with fan, also male and female dorms (US$13), camping (US$9), pool table, TV lounge, small kitchen, arrange visits to the falls; website has detailed instructions for how to reach them.

Restaurants

$$$ Búfalo Branco
R Rebouças 530, T045-3523 9744, http://bufalobranco.com.br.
Superb all you can eat *churrasco*, includes filet mignon, bull's testicles, salad bar and desert. Sophisticated surroundings and attentive service. Highly recommended.

$$$ Rafain
Av das Cataratas 1749, T045-3523 1177, www.rafainchurrascaria.com.br. Closed Sun evening.
Out of town, take a taxi or arrange with travel agency. Set price for excellent buffet with folkloric music and dancing (2100-2300), touristy but very entertaining. Recommended.

$$$ Zaragoza
R Quintino Bocaiúva 882, T045-3028 8084, http://restaurantezaragoza.com.br.
Large and upmarket, for Spanish dishes and seafood. Recommended.

$$ Atos
Av Juscelino Kubitschek 865, T045-3572 2785.
Per kilo buffet with various meats, salads, sushi and puddings. Lunch only.

$$ Bier Garten
Av Jorge Schimmelpfeng 550, T045-3523 3700, Facebook: Bier Garten.
Bustling pizzeria, *churrascaria* and *choperia*.

Cafés

Marias e Maria
Av Brasil 505, T045-3523 5472, http://mariasemaria.com.br.
Established *confeitaria* with good savouries and sweets.

Oficina do Sorvete
Av Jorge Schimmelpfeng 244. Daily 1100-0100.
Excellent ice creams, a popular local hang-out.

Bars and clubs

Bars, all doubling as restaurants, concentrated on Av Jorge Schimmelpfeng for 2 blocks from Av Brasil to R Mal Floriano Peixoto. Wed to Sun are best nights; crowd tends to be young.

Armazém
R Edmundo de Barros 458, T045-3572 0007, www.armazemrestaurante.com.br.
Intimate and sophisticated, attracts discerning locals, good atmosphere, mellow live music. Recommended.

Capitão Bar
Av Jorge Schimmelpfeng 288 and Almte Barroso, T045-3572 1512, http:// capitaobar.com.
Large, loud and popular, nightclub attached.

Oba! Oba!
Av Mercosul 400, T045-3529 9070, www.obaobasambashow.com.br. At Churrascaria Bottega. Daily 1200-1530 for lunch, Mon-Sat 2000-2200.
With live samba show at 2200.

Pizza Park Bar
R Almirante Barroso 993.
Specializes in vodka and whisky brands. Wi-Fi zone.

What to do

There are many travel agents on Av Brasil. Lots of companies on both sides organize conventional tours to the falls, useful more for convenience rather than information, since they collect you from your hotel. Confirm whether all entrance fees are included. Beware of overcharging by touts at the bus terminal.

Parque Nacional Foz do Iguaçu
Tours

Guayi Travel, *R Irian Kalichewiski 265, Vila Yolanda, T045-3027 0043, www. guayitravel.com.* Excellent tours to both sides of the falls, Ciudad del Este, Itaipu and around, including options for birders and wildlife enthusiasts. English and Spanish spoken.

Macuco Safari, *T045-3529 6262, or T045-99963 3857, www.macucosafari.com. br.* 2 hrs, US$50, involves a ride down a 1.5-km path through the forest in open jeeps and an optional walk. Then a fast motor boat whisks you close to the falls themselves (in the same vein as Jungle Explorer on the Argentine side). Portuguese, English and Spanish spoken, take insect repellent and waterproof camera bag.

Transport

Parque Nacional Foz do Iguaçu
Bus Buses leave from the Terminal Urbana in Foz, Av Juscelino Kubitschek and República Argentina, every 40 mins from 0730-1800, and are clearly marked 'Parque Nacional'. You can get on or off at any point on the route past the airport and **Hotel das Cataratas**, 40 mins, US$1.35 one way, payable in reais or pesos (bus route ends at the park entrance where you purchase entry tickets and change to a park bus).

Foz do Iguaçu
Air Aeroporto Internacional de Cataratas, BR 469, Km 16.5, 13 km east of the centre and 12 km from the falls, T045-3521 4200. In Arrivals are ATMs and **Caribe Tours e Câmbio**, car rental offices, tourist office and an official taxi stand, US$17.50 to town centre. All buses marked Parque Nacional pass the airport in each direction, US$1.35, 0525-0040, does not permit large amounts of luggage but backpacks OK. Many hotels run minibus services for a small charge. Daily flights to **Rio**, **São Paulo**, **Curitiba** and other Brazilian cities.

Bus For transport to the falls see above. The *rodoviária* long-distance terminal, Av Costa e Silva, is 4 km from centre on road to Curitiba, T045-3522 3633; bus to centre from next to the taxis, US$1. Taxi US$8. Book departures as soon as possible. As well as the tourist office, there is Guarda Municipal (police), Visa ATM, and luggage store. To **Curitiba**, 9-10 hrs, paved road, US$45. To **Florianópolis**, US$45-53, 14 hrs. **Unesul** to **Porto Alegre**, US$45-51. To **São Paulo**, 16 hrs, US$34-58. To **Campo Grande**, US$44. Local buses leave from the **Terminal de Transporte Urbano**, TTU on Av Juscelino Kubitscheck and passengers can buy pre-paid cards, US$1 per journey (it costs more if you don't have a card). Services called *alimentador* in the suburbs are free.

Foz do Iguaçu and around: Itaipu dam

Bus Take bus lines Conjunto C Norte or Conjunto C Sul from Foz do Iguaçu Terminal de Transporte Urbano, US$0.75.

Border with Argentina: Foz do Iguaçu/ Puerto Iguazú

Bus Buses marked 'Puerto Iguazú' run every 30 mins Mon-Sat, hourly on Sun, from the Terminal Urbana, crossing the border bridge; 30 mins' journey, 3 companies, US$2. See above for procedures regarding entry stamps.

Note Be sure you know when the last bus departs from Puerto Iguazú for Foz (usually 1900); last bus from Foz 1950. If visiting the Brazilian side for a day, get off the bus at the Hotel Bourbon, cross the road and catch the bus to the falls, rather than going into Foz and out again. Combined tickets to Puerto Iguazú and the falls cost more than paying separately.

Border with Paraguay: Foz do Iguaçu/ Ciudad del Este

Bus Buses marked 'Cidade-Ponte' leave from the Terminal Urbana, Av Juscelino Kubitschek, for the Ponte de Amizade (Friendship Bridge), US$1.20. To **Asunción**, Pluma (0700), **Nuestra Señora de la Asunción**, from *rodoviária*, about US$15 (more options from Ciudad del Este).

Car If crossing by private vehicle and only intending to visit the national parks, this presents no problems. Another crossing to Paraguay is at **Guaíra**, at the northern end of the Itaipu lake. It is 5 hrs north of Iguaçu by road and can be reached by bus from Campo Grande and São Paulo. Ferries cross to Saltos del Guaira on the Paraguayan side.

Argentine side of the falls
get up close to the waterfalls and explore the rainforest trails

Parque Nacional Iguazú covers an area of 67,620 ha. The fauna includes jaguars, tapirs, brown capuchin monkeys, collared anteaters and coatimundis, although these are rarely seen around the falls. There is a huge variety of birds. Among the butterfly species are shiny blue morphos and red/black heliconius.

Parque Nacional Iguazú

T3757-491469, www.iguazuargentina.com. The park is open daily 0800-1800; last access 1630. Tickets cost US$28 (children 6-12 US$7), payable in Argentine pesos only. Credit and debit card can be used once inside the park, but not for the entrance and parking tickets. From the bus terminal in Puerto Iguazú, buses run to the park roughly every 20 mins daily 0700-2050.

From the visitor centre a small gas-run train (free), the **Tren de la Selva**, whisks visitors on a 25-minute trip through the jungle to the Estación del Diablo, where it's a 1-km walk along catwalks across the Río Iguazú to the park's centrepiece, the **Garanta del Diablo**. A visit here is particularly recommended in the evening when the light is best and the swifts are returning to roost on the cliffs, some behind the water. Trains leave on the hour and on the half hour. However, it's best to see the falls from a distance first, with excellent views from the two well-organized trails along the Circuito Superior and Circuito Inferior, each taking around an hour and a half. To reach these, get off the train at the Estación Cataratas (after 10 minutes' journey) and walk down the **Sendero Verde**. The **Circuito Superior** is a level path which takes you along the easternmost line of falls, Bossetti, Bernabé Mandez, Mbiguá (Guaraní for cormorant) and San Martín, allowing you to see these falls from above. This path is safe for those with walking difficulties, wheelchairs and pushchairs, though you should wear supportive non-slippery shoes. The **Circuito Inferior** takes you down to the water's edge via a series of steep stairs and walkways with superb views of both San Martín falls and the Gaganta del Diablo from a distance. Wheelchair users, pram pushers, and those who aren't good with steps should go down by the exit route for a smooth and easy descent. You could then return to the Estación Cataratas to take the train to Estación Garganta, which leaves at 10 and 40 minutes past the hour, and see the falls close up. Every month on the five nights of full moon, there are 1½-hour guided walks (bilingual) that may include a dinner before or after the walk, at the **Restaurant La Selva**. See the park website for dates, times and email booking form; reservations can also be made in person at the park, or through agencies: US$68 with dinner; US$50 without.

③ **Puerto Iguazú**

⇒ Iguazú Falls
1 Around Iguazú Falls, page 80
2 Foz do Iguaçu, page 83
3 **Puerto Iguazú, page 89**

Where to stay
1 Garden Stone
2 Hostería Casa Blanca
3 Iguazú Jungle Lodge
4 Marco Polo Inn
8 Noelia
5 Panoramic
6 Peter Pan
10 Secret Garden

Restaurants
1 Aqva
2 El Quincho del Tío Querido
5 La Rueda
6 Pizza Color
8 Tango Bar Iguazú

At the very bottom of the Circuito Inferior, a free ferry crosses 0930-1530 on demand to the small, hilly **Isla San Martín** where trails lead to miradores with good close views of the **San Martín Falls**. The park has two further trails: **Sendero Macuco**, 7 km return (the park says two to three hours, but allow much more), starting from near the visitor centre and leading to the river via a natural pool (El Pozón) fed by a slender waterfall, **Salto Arrechea** (a good place for bathing and the only permitted place in the park). **Sendero Yacaratiá** starts from the same place, but reaches the river by a different route, and ends at Puerto Macuco, where you could take the *Jungle Explorer* boat to the see the falls themselves (see below). This trail is really for vehicles (30 km in total) and is best visited on an organized safari.

Puerto Iguazú

This modern town (population 41,062) is 18 km northwest of the falls high above the river on the Argentine side near the confluence of the Río Iguazú and Río Paraná. It serves mainly as a centre for visitors to the falls. The port lies to the north of the town centre at the foot of a hill. From the port you can follow the Río Iguazú downstream towards Hito-Tres Fronteras, a mirador with views over the point where the Río Iguazú and Río Paraná meet and over neighbouring Brazil and Paraguay. There are souvenir shops, toilets and pubs here; bus US$0.50. **La Aripuca** ⓘ *turn off Ruta 12 just after Hotel Cataratas, entrance after 250 m, T3757-423488, www.aripuca.com.ar, US$3, 0900-1800, English and German spoken*, is a large wooden structure housing a centre for the appreciation of the native tree species and their environment. The **Güirá Oga**, also known as the **Casa de los Pájaros** ⓘ *turn off Ruta 12 at Hotel Orquídeas Palace, entrance is 800 m further along the road from Aripuca, T3757-423980, www.guiraoga.fundacionazara.org.ar, US$2, daily 0830-1830*, is a sanctuary where injured birds are treated and reintroduced to the wild. Species include exquisite parrots and magnificent birds of prey. There is also a trail in the forest and a breeding centre for endangered species.

Listings Argentine side of the falls *map p89*

Tourist information

As well as the visitor centre at the falls, information is available from:
Tourist office, *Av Victoria Aguirre 396, Puerto Iguazú, T03757-420800.*
Municipal office, *Av Victoria Aguirre y Balbino Brañas, T03757-422938, 0900-2200, www.iguazuturismo.gov.ar.*
National park office, *Victoria Aguirre 66, T03757-420722, iguazu@apn.gov.ar.*

Where to stay

$$$$ Panoramic
Paraguay 372, T0800-999 4726, www.panoramic-hoteliguazu.com.
On a hill overlooking the river, this hotel is stunning. Serene outdoor pool with great views, large well-designed rooms and all 5-star inclusions.

$$$$ Posada Puerto Bemberg
Fundadores Bemberg s/n, Puerto Libertad (some 35 km south of Iguazú), T03757-

496500, www.puertobemberg.com.
Wonderful luxury accommodation and
gourmet cuisine in Posada and **Casa
Puerto Bemberg**, dating from 1940s,
surrounded by lush gardens. Huge living
areas, beautifully decorated rooms
and helpful staff. Good birdwatching
with resident naturalist. Highly
recommended.

**$$$$ Sheraton Internacional
Iguazú Resort**
*T03757-491800,
www.sheraton.com/iguazu.*
Fine position overlooking the falls,
excellent, good restaurant and breakfast,
sports facilities and spa. Taxi to airport
available. Recommended.

$$$$ Yacutinga Lodge
*30 km from town, pick-up by jeep,
www.yacutinga.com.*
A beautiful lodge in the middle of the
rainforest, with 2- to 4-night packages,
learning about the bird and plant life
and Guaraní culture. Accommodation
is in rustic adobe houses in tropical
gardens, superb food and drinks
included, as well as boat trips and
walks. Contact by email.

$$$ Iguazú Jungle Lodge
*Hipólito Iyrigoyen y San Lorenzo, T03757-
420600, www.iguazujunglelodge.com.*
A well-designed complex of lofts and
family suites, 7 blocks from the centre,
by a river, with lovely pool. Comfortable
and stylish, DVDs, great service,
restaurant. Warmly recommended.

$$$ Posada 21 Oranges
*C Montecarlo y Av los Inmigrantes,
T03757-494014, www.21oranges.com.*
10 simple but comfortable rooms
set around a pool, lovely garden,
welcoming. US$5 taxi ride or 20-min
walk to town.

$$$ Secret Garden
*Los Lapachos 623, T03757-423099,
www.secretgardeniguazu.com.*
Small B&B with attentive owner, fern
garden surrounding the house. Spacious
rooms, good breakfast and cocktails,
relaxing atmosphere.

$$$-$$ Hostería Casa Blanca
*Guaraní 121, near bus station, T03757-
421320, www.casablancaiguazu.com.ar.*
Family-run, large rooms, good showers,
beautifully maintained.

$ pp Garden Stone
*Av Córdoba 441, T03757-420425,
www.gardenstonehostel.com.*
Lovely hostel with a homely feel
set in nice gardens, with a large
outdoor eating area, swimming pool.
Recommended for a tranquil stay.

$ pp Hostel Inn Iguazú
*R 12, Km 5, T03757-421823,
http://hiiguazu.com.*
20% discount to HI members and 10%
discount on long-distance buses, dorms
US$13, a/c doubles **$$**. Large, well-
organized hostel which used to be a
casino. Huge pool, games and a range of
free DVDs to watch. They also organize
package tours to the falls, which include
accommodation. No guests under 18.

$ pp Marco Polo Inn
*Av Córdoba 154, T03757-425559,
www.marcopoloinniguazu.com.*
The biggest and most central hostel in
town, right in front of the bus station, a/c
doubles **$$**. Nice pool, fun bar at night
(open to non-residents). It gets busy so
reserve in advance. Recommended.

$ pp Noelia
Fray Luis Beltrán 119, T03757-420729, www.hostelnoelia.com.
Cheap, well-kept and helpful, good breakfast, family-run, good value.

$ pp Peter Pan
Av Córdoba 267, T03757-423616, www.peterpanhostel.com.
Just down the hill from the bus station, spotless, central pool and large open kitchen. The doubles ($$) are lovely. Helpful staff.

Restaurants

$$ Aqva
Av Córdoba y Carlos Thays, T03757-422064, www.aqvarestaurant.com.
Just down from the bus station, this lovely restaurant serves dishes made with ingredients from the area.

$$ El Quincho del Tío Querido
Perón and Caraguatá, T03757-420151, www.eltioquerido.com.ar.
Recommended for *parrilla* and local fish, very popular, great value.

$$ La Rueda
Córdoba 28, T03757-422531, www.larueda1975.com.ar.
Good food and prices, fish, steaks and pastas, often with mellow live music. Highly recommended.

$$ Pizza Color
Córdoba 135, T03757-420206, www.parrillapizzacolor.com.
Popular for pizza and *parrilla*.

$$ Tango Bar Iguazú
Av Brasil 1, T03757-422008.
Bar which serves pizzas and pastas. It turns into a *milonga* with tango classes and dancing at night.

What to do

Agencies arrange day tours to the Brazilian side (lunch in Foz), Itaipú and Ciudad del Este. Some include the duty free mall on the Argentine side. Tours to the Jesuit ruins at San Ignacio Miní also visit a gem mine at Wanda (you don't see as much of the ruins as you do if staying overnight).

Agroturismo Sombra de Toro, *Ruta Nacional 101, Bernardo de Yrigoyen, T03757-15-449425.* By the Parque Provincial Urugua-í, which adjoins the Iguazú national park, this farm owned by the Mackoviak family offers tours and accommodation on their private reserve, which contains Selva Paranaense and examples of the rare *sombra de toro* tree.

Iguazú Falls tours

Aguas Grandes, *Mariano Moreno 58, T03757-425500, www.aguasgrandes. com.* Tours to both sides of the falls and further afield, activities in the forest, abseiling down waterfalls, good fun.

Explorador Expediciones, *Perito Moreno 217, T03757 491469, www. rainforest.iguazuargentina.com.* Offers small-group tours: **Safari a la Cascada** which takes you by jeep to the Arrechea waterfall, stopping along the way to look at wildlife, with a short walk to the falls, 2 hrs. And **Safari en la Selva**, more in-depth interpretation of the wildlife all around, in open jeeps, 2 hrs. Highly recommended. They also run 3-day packages, birdwatching trips, adventure tours, tours to Moconá. Recommended.

Jungle Explorer, *T03757-421696, www. iguazujungle.com.* Runs a series of boat trips, all highly recommended.

Aventura Náutica is an exhilarating journey by launch along the lower Río Iguazú, from opposite Isla San Martín right up to the San Martín falls and then into the Garganta del Diablo, completely drenching passengers in the mighty spray; great fun but not for the faint-hearted. On **Paseo Ecológico** you float silently for 2.5 km from Estación Garganta to appreciate the wildlife on the river banks, 30 mins, US$31.

Transport

Puerto Iguazú
Air Airport is 20 km southeast of Puerto Iguazú near the falls, T03757-422013. The **Four Tourist Travel** bus service runs between the airport and the bus terminal, US$6, and will also drop off/collect from your hotel. Taxi US$15.

Bus For transport to the falls see above under Parque Nacional Iguazú. The bus terminal, at Av Córdoba y Av Misiones, T03757-423006, has a telephone office, restaurant, various tour company desks and bus offices. To **Buenos Aires**, 16-18 hrs, **Tigre Iguazú** and others, via Bariloche, daily, US$115-129. To **Posadas**, stopping at **San Ignacio Miní**, frequent, 5-6 hrs, US$17-20; to **San Ignacio Miní**, US$17-20. **Agencia de Pasajes Noelia**, local 3, T03757-422722, can book tickets beyond Posadas for other destinations in Argentina. ISIC discounts available.

Taxi T03757-420973. Fares in town US$2.50-4.

Border with Brazil
Crossing via the Puente Tancredo Neves is straightforward. When leaving Argentina, Argentine immigration is at the Brazilian end of the bridge. Border open 0700-2300. Brazilian consulate, Av Córdoba 264, T03757-420192, conbrasil@iguazunet.com.

Bus Buses leave Puerto Iguazú terminal for **Foz do Iguaçu** every 15 mins, 0730-1830, US$1.25. The bus stops at the Argentine border post, but not the Brazilian. Both Argentine and Brazilian officials stamp you in and out, even if only for a day visit. Whether you are entering Brazil for the first time, or leaving and returning after a day in Argentina, you must insist on getting off the bus to get the required stamp and entry card. Buses also stop at the Duty Free mall. The bus does not wait for those who need stamps, just catch the next one.

Taxi Between the border and Puerto Iguazú US$25.

Border with Paraguay
Crossing to Paraguay is via Puente Tancredo Neves to Brazil and then via the Puente de la Amistad to Ciudad del Este. Brazilian entry and exit stamps are not required unless you are stopping in Brazil, but you must have them from Argentina (and a visa if you need one) to enter Paraguay. The Paraguayan consulate is at Puerto Moreno 236, T03757-424230, Mon-Fri 0800-1600.

Bus Direct buses (non-stop in Brazil), leave Puerto Iguazú terminal every 40 mins, US$4.50, 45 mins, liable to delays especially in crossing the bridge to Ciudad del Este. Only 1 bus on Sun, no schedule, better to go to Foz and change buses there.

Ferry There is a ferry service (US$3 pp, US$5.75 per auto) from the port in Puerto Iguazú to Tres Fronteras. It has an immigration check and is a popular crossing for those without a Brazilian visa who wish to only travel between Argentina and Paraguay.

North of Asunción

The winding Río Paraguay is 400 m wide and is still a major trade route for the products of northern Paraguay, although it is fast losing out to the paved highway (Ruta 5) built to Concepción and accessible from either side of the river. Even so, with the start of the rainy season, some farms and rural communities lose their overland connection to the outside world. Boats carry cattle, hides, yerba mate, tobacco and timber, much of which comes from Mennonite colonies and, further north, vast estancias. This is an infrequently visited region for the traveller, who, with some patience and flexibility, will be rewarded by the sight of several species of flora and fauna not easily found elsewhere, as well as a number of rarely accessed national parks and scenic reserves.

Best for
Estancias ▪ National parks ▪ River trips

Travelling north from Asunción by river (nowadays mostly done in an upscale version of a cargo boat with a few sleeping cabins) is fairly straightforward. Before leaving it's a good idea to get any necessary exit stamps in Asunción if planning to travel to Bolivia or Brazil, as they are not always available in Concepción and further north (no matter what you may be told).

By boat All river trips start from the bay, so you'll first come across Puente Remanso in neighbouring Mariano Roque Alonso, the bridge that marks the beginning of the Trans-Chaco Highway (Ruta 9). Just further upstream is **Villa Hayes**, 31 km above Asunción, founded in 1786 but renamed in 1879 after US President Rutherford Hayes, who arbitrated a territorial dispute with Argentina in Paraguay's favour. Further upstream at 198 km is **Puerto Antequera**. Boats often stop here, and if so and you have a flexible itinerary, you can catch a bus (US$2.50) 15 km east along Ruta 11 to **San Pedro del Ycuamandiyú**, the only significant town north of Villa Hayes until Concepción anywhere near the Río Paraguay. It has a pleasant centre with colonial-era buildings, a church constructed in the Jesuit style (although after their expulsion in 1767) and the nearby Río Jejui is a nice place to spend an afternoon swimming or camping. By boat, some 100 km beyond Puerto Antequera is Concepción. All travellers arriving by boat from Asunción should disembark at the Administración Nacional de Navegación just before the bridge.

By road By road there are two alternative routes. One is via the Trans-Chaco Highway (269 km along Ruta 9 from Asunción) and then right at the petrol station in **Pozo Colorado**, a total journey of a good five to seven hours in normal circumstances. The Pozo Colorado–Concepción road (Carretera General Bernardino Caballero), 146 km, is completely paved and offers spectacular views of birdlife. Many consider it the best, easily accessed spot in Paraguay for seeing wildlife.

The other route, also fully paved, is Ruta 3, starting in Mariano Roque Alonso, to **Yby Yaú** (339 km) and then west along Ruta 5 (110 km, or seven to nine hours in all from Asunción) to Concepción.

Mennonite and German colonies

There are a number of Swiss-German and Mennonite communities in the area between San Estanislao and San Pedro Ycuamandiyú (eg Colonia Volendam, Tacuruty and the controversial settlement of Nueva Alemania), with bus service from both towns as well as from Asunción. Most of these colonias have no formal accommodation. The land here is mostly given over to farming manioc and yerba mate and the climate is oppressively hot year-round. At **Santa Rosa del Aguaray** (not a colonia), 108 km north of San Estanislao, there is a bank, petrol, *pensión* and restaurants, but little else in the area.

From Santa Rosa del Aguaray, a paved road (Ruta 11) runs southwest for 27 km to **Nueva Germania**, founded in 1866 by Bernhard Förster and Elisabeth

Nietzsche (the philosopher's sister) to establish a pure Aryan colony (follow signs to **Hotel Germania**, $ with air conditioning, very clean). Nueva Germania, which until recently flew a German flag from the town's entrance, was allegedly the hideout for the notorious Nazi Josef Mengele after his disappearance from another German settlement, Hohenau, outside Encarnación (see page 53). From Nueva Germania, the road goes on to San Pedro del Ycuamandiyú (48 km), and Puerto Antequera (see above) on the Río Paraguay (another 14 km). East of Santa Rosa del Aguaray, 23 km, is $ **Rancho Laguna Blanca** (T021-424760 in Asunción or T981-558671, www.lagunablanca.com.py, day visits US$3.50, camping US$5.25, dormitory US$17.50 for one person), a nature reserve, family farm and rural tourism centre offering lots of activities including riding, trekking, kayaking, birdwatching and just lolling about on the lake's beach (which is so well maintained it looks as if it belongs in the Caribbean). It is one of the few facilities in this area open year-round. Next door is the **Para la Tierra Foundation** ⓘ *T985-260074, www.paralatierra.org*, which works to support environmental tourism and research and welcomes visitors. A further 23 km north of Santa Rosa, a dirt road runs northeast through jungle for 105 km to the interesting town of **Capitán Badó**, which forms the frontier with Brazil. About 50 km north of the turn-off to Capitán Badó is Yby Yaú (see page 101). From Capitán Badó a road follows the frontier north to Pedro Juan Caballero (another 119 km, see page 102).

Listings Asunción to Concepción

From the west: Pozo Colorado

$$ Buffalo Bill
Km 283 (3 km northwest of turn onto Ruta 5), T991-866780.
Famous restaurant with a lake and small zoo. The best place in the Chaco.

$$-$ Parador del Touring y Automóvil Club
Km 270 (a few kilometres before the turn onto Ruta 5), T971-395750, www.tacpy.com.py. Friendly, clean and inexpensive.
Good food and a scenic setting.

$ Parador Pirahú
Km 249, T991-700683.
No frills, but clean and efficient. Best bet if not wanting to stay in or around town.

From the east: Mennonite and German colonies

$ Hotel Waldbrunner
Colonia Volendam, T0451-320175, www.hotel-waldbrunner.de.
Bath, cheaper without a/c, also has a good restaurant, extremely clean, very helpful. German spoken.

South of Concepción: Cruce Liberación

$$$ Estancia Jejui
Set on the Río Jejui, 65 km north of Tacuara on Ruta 3, address in Asunción, Telmo Aquino 4068, T021-600227, http://jejui.coinco.com.py.
All rooms with a/c, bathroom and hot water, full board, fishing, horse riding, tennis, boat rides extra.

Concepción (population 60,346), 422 km north of Asunción via Ruta 9 and Ruta 5 (or 439 km via Ruta 3), stands on the east bank of the Río Paraguay. Founded by Agustín de Pinedo in 1773 as a base of military operations for exploration of the Chaco, it is known as 'La Perla del Norte' for its climate and setting, both of which are considered better than almost anywhere else this far north in Paraguay.

To appreciate the colonial aspect of the city, walk away from the main commercial streets. Sunsets from the port are beautiful. At Plaza La Libertad are the cathedral and the Municipalidad. Main services are on Pdte Franco, such as post, telephone, internet, ATMs and exchange (eg **Norte Cambios** ① *Pdte Franco y 14 de Mayo, www. nortecambios.com.py, Mon-Fri 0830-1700, Sat 0830-1100, fair rates for US$ and euros, cash only*; **Financiera Familiar** ① *Pdte Franco y General Garay, US$ cash only*.

Throughout the town there are remnants of its successful past as a commercial centre in the form of large houses and other buildings constructed in decidedly belle-époque European style. Many of these edifices were preserved by later generations of Italian, Lebanese and Spanish immigrants arriving in Concepción in the 1930s and 1940s, and the town still has an eclectic feel to it. Sunsets from the port are beautiful. The town is the trade centre of the north, doing considerable business with Brazil. The **Brazilian consulate** ① *Av Pdte Franco 972, T0331-242655, vc.concepcion@itamaraty.gov.br, Mon-Fri 0800-1400, issues visas*, but go early to ensure same-day processing.

Sights
The picturesque market, a good place to try local food, is east of the main street, **Agustín de Pinedo** (which is a kind of open-air museum, the **Museo de Arqueología Industrial**, with antique railway cars and agricultural machines lining sections of the street). From here Avenida Presidente Franco runs west to the port. Along Avenida Agustín de Pinedo is a large statue of María Auxiliadora with the Christ Child. There are stairs to balconies at the base of the monument which offer good views.

The **Museo Municipal Ex-Cuartal Militar** ① *Mcal López, in the same 19th-century building as the Teatro Municipal and diagonally opposite the Municipalidad, T971-803951, www.portalguarani.com (under 'Museums and cultural centres'), Mon-Sat 0700-1200, free*, contains a dusty collection of local items and faded photographs, most of which portray either the War of the Triple Alliance or the Chaco War. You must ask for it to be opened as it's worth a look. The library is also surprisingly interesting.

The **Biblioteca Municipal** ① *Mansión Quevedo, Mcal López, T0331-853779, www.portalguarani.com (under 'Museums and cultural centres'), Mon-Fri 0700-1200 and 1300-1700, free*, has a contemporary art exhibit (rare for any city outside of Asunción or Villarrica), and offers dance, music and theatre performances. But its real gem is the small museum which, like the Museo Ex-Cuartal Militar, above, is open upon request only. It's hard to say what it's all about; it most closely resembles a curio shop of the Victorian era. Everything from furniture from the colonial period to Guaraní mission sculpture to the country's first piano and an early television set are crammed into four rooms and well worth the effort to see. The city historian, Sr Medina, offers good sightseeing tours; ask for him.

Plaza Agustín Fernando de Pinedo has a permanent craft market. Much of the centre of Concepción can be seen from a *karumbé* tour (US$3.50).

Around Concepción

Downriver from the town, about 9 km south is a bridge across the Río Paraguay, which makes for an interesting walk across the shallows and islands to the west bank and the Chaco, about an hour return trip, taxi US$10. At weekends, the top of the bridge becomes a party venue for the city's youth. For more information visit the town's website, www.concepcion-py.com.

The large island in the Río Paraguay facing Concepción is **Isla Chaco'i**, a planned free-trade zone and tourism complex but at present largely uninhabited, where you can stroll through the fields. Rowing boats take passengers to the island from the shore next to the port, US$0.50 per person. Some 17 km to the northeast on Ruta Teniente Avalos is a little-known national park, **Arroyo Yu'i-y**, wonderful for hiking through a buffer zone between the 'Humid' Chaco and Pantanal ecosystems.

Listings Concepción

Where to stay

$$$ Concepción Palace
Mcal López 399 y E A Garay, T0331-241858, www.concepcionpalace.com.py.
By far the nicest hotel in town. With all mod cons, pool, restaurant, Wi-Fi throughout, large rooms.

$$-$ Francés
Franco y C A López, T0331-242383, www.hotelfrancesconcepcion.com.
With a/c, cheaper with fan, breakfast, nice grounds with pool (small charge for non-guests), restaurant, parking.

$$-$ pp Granja El Roble
In Dieciseis (16 km from Concepción on road to Belén), T985-898446, www.paraguay.ch.
Working farm and nature reserve with various sleeping options, full board with homegrown food, camping US$7, lots of activities including boat trips,

tubing on Río Ypané, tours to the Chaco, aquarium, very good bird and wildlife-watching (special trips arranged, including for scientists), local information including on routes to Bolivia, internet, Wi-Fi. Excellent value, prices are not negotiable. Phone in advance to arrange transport if required.

$ Center
Presidente Franco e Yegros, T0331-242360.
More basic and cheaper than others, popular.

$ Concepción
Don Bosco y Cabral near market, T0331-242506.
With simple breakfast, a/c, cheaper with fan, family run, good value.

$ Victoria
Franco y PJ Caballero 693, T0331-242256, hotelvictoria@hotmail.es.

Pleasant rooms, a/c, fridge, cheaper with fan, restaurant, parking.

Restaurants

$ Hotel Francés
See Where to stay, above.
Good-value buffet lunch, à la carte in the evening.

$ Hotel Victoria
See Where to stay, above.
Set lunches and à la carte, grill in *quincho* across the street.

$ Palo Santo
Franco y PJ Caballero, T0331-241454.
Good Brazilian food and value.

$ Ysapy
Yegros y Mcal Estigarribia at Plaza Pineda. Daily 1630-0200.
Pizza and icecream, terrace or sidewalk seating, very popular.

Transport

Boat To/from **Asunción**, the only boat taking passengers is the *Guaraní*, which has a 2-week sailing cycle on the Asunción–Fuerte Olimpo route and is very slow, but nice and welcomes tourists. To make arrangements for the boat, speak to the owner and captain, Julio Desvares, T982-873436, or Don Coelo, T972-678695. To **Bahía Negra** and intermediate points along the upper Río Paraguay, the *Aquidabán* sails Tue 1100, arriving Bahía Negra on Fri morning and returns the same day to Concepción, arriving on Sun, US$17.50 to Bahía Negra, US$17.50 for a berth (book by the Fri of the week before, at least). If you don't want a berth, take a hammock. Meals are sold on board (US$2.20), but best to take food and water. Tickets sold in office just outside the port,

T0331-242435, Mon-Sat 0700-1200. From Bahía Negra to **Puerto Suárez** (Bolivia) you must hire a boat to Puerto Busch, about US$85-95, then catch a bus. There are sporadic ferries from Concepción to Isla Margarita, across from Porto Murtinho, Brazil. Ask for prices and times at dock and note that service does not include anything other than standing room. A regular ferry, for 1 vehicle and a few passengers, US$44 per vehicle, goes between Capitán Carmelo Peralta (customs and immigration service at west end of town) and Porto Murtinho (no immigration, head for Ponta Porã, Corumbá or Campo Grande; obtain visa in advance). **Note** If planning to go to Bolivia or Brazil by this route, you must enquire before arriving at the border, even in Asunción, about exit and entry formalities. Visas for either country must be obtained in advance. There is an immigration office in Concepción (see above), but not further towards Brazil.

Bus The terminal is on the outskirts, 8 blocks north along General Garay, but buses also stop in the centre, Av Pinedo, look for signs Parada Omnibus. A shuttle bus (Línea 1) runs between the terminal and the port. Taxi from terminal or port to centre, US$4; terminal to port US6. To **Asunción**, many daily with **Nasa-Golondrina** (T0331-242744), 3 with **La Santaniana**, plus other companies, US$10.50-12, 5½ hrs via Pozo Colorado, 9 hrs via Coronel Oviedo. To **Pedro Juan Caballero**, frequent service, several companies, US$10, 4-5 hrs. To **Horqueta**, 1 hr, US$2.50. To **Filadelfia**, **Nasa-Golondrina** direct at 0730 Mon, Sat, US$12, 5 hrs, otherwise change at Pozo Colorado. To **Ciudad del Este**, **García** direct at 1230 daily, US$22, 9 hrs, or change at Coronel Oviedo.

One of the more appealing notions of travel in Paraguay is the thought of a leisurely cruise along the Río Paraguay, starting in Asunción and eventually reaching Puerto Busch in the Bolivian Pantanal.

It is best to break the trip into three stages: from Asunción to Concepción (see above); from Concepción to Bahía Negra; and from Bahía Negra to Puerto Busch. There is no unbroken voyage between the three points, and upriver travel will need to be confirmed for the next stage of the journey, in both Concepción (to Bahía Negra but no further) and Bahía Negra (to Puerto Busch).

Although you may be able to get an exit stamp (for onward travel to Bolivia or Brazil) as far upriver as Colonia Peralta or Fuerte Olimpo (both below Bahía Negra), these towns are very small and you'll probably pass through them at night when everything is closed. You cannot get an exit stamp at Bahía Negra. Your best bet is to get it in Concepción or possibly in Asunción at the **Departamento de Identificaciones** ⓘ *Rl2 Ytororo y Hassler, T021-605618, Mon-Fri 0700-1900, Sat 0700-1200*. Although you may be directed to Concepción, there are reports of some visitors receiving their exit stamps in Asunción.

Visitors from the United States and Israel must obtain an actual visa (US$160 if obtained in a Bolivian consulate in the US; otherwise it costs US$135. For Israelis it's US$135), in addition to an exit stamp, in Asunción (the only other option is Ciudad del Este) in order to enter Bolivian territory. Bolivian authorities are inflexible in this matter; do not take risks.

To make the journey, once in Concepción find the *Aquidabán* (T0331-242435), a cargo boat that leaves every Tuesday at 1100 from the port (a few kilometres north of the bridge, in the area that runs parallel with Nanawa near its intersection with Brasil) to Bahía Negra. Weather permitting, it arrives in Bahía Negra late Thursday morning. The only towns of any note you will pass along the river en route are **Villemí** and **Fuerte Olimpo**. The cost is US$27.50 per person, and a cabin – of which there are only a few, so book some days in advance – costs an extra US$27.50. Meals are US$2.50, although enquire ahead of time to make sure they are provided as on some cruises they are not. The scenery is enjoyable, but the journey is usually cramped and very not comfortable. Bring plenty of water, a hat, mosquito netting and sun screen. At Bahía Negra you will need to disembark, as the *Aquidabán* returns to Concepción the following day.

If you opt for another craft in Concepción (such as the *Guaraní*), it will be a no-frills affair with fewer amenities than the *Aquidibán*. As a minimum you'll need a hammock (no other boats have private cabins), mosquito screen, food and water. Expect to pay US$17.50 pp, US$17.50 for berth and US$2.20 meals for the one-way journey, arriving in Bahía Negra 36-48 hours later. If the *Aquidabán* is not your transport, make absolutely certain that your boat will travel as far as at least Villemí or, better still, Fuerte Olimpo, as no other riverine communities outside of Bahía Negra offer a service to Bolivia.

ON THE ROAD

Hammocks

A hammock can be an invaluable piece of equipment, especially if travelling on the cheap, along the rivers or in the Chaco. It will be of more use than a tent because many places have hammock hooks, or you can sling a hammock between trees or posts. A good tip is to carry a length of rope and some plastic sheeting. The rope gives a good choice of tree distances and the excess provides a hanging frame for the plastic sheeting to keep the rain off. Metal S-hooks or a couple of climbing karabiners can also be very useful, as can strong cord for tying out the sheeting. Don't forget a mosquito net if travelling in insect-infected areas.

If a stop in Villemí can be arranged, it is worth exploring one of Paraguay's more successful municipal tourism initiatives in the area. A tributary of the Río Paraguay, the Río Apa, which for some kilometres forms the border between Paraguay and Brazil, is now the site of an ambitious tour offering sponsored by the **Municipalidad** ⓘ *13 de Junio y Río Apa, T985-170952*.

From Bahía Negra there are boats to Puerto Busch in Bolivia, although you'll have to ask around for them, as well as negotiate the cost of the voyage, which is generally about US$85-95. The trip takes another 24 hours as the channel is much shallower as you approach the Pantanal and its myriad streams and islands.

East of Concepción

spectacular park with steep forested hills, caves and petroglyphs

There is a 215-km road (Ruta 5, fully paved) from Concepción, eastwards to the Brazilian border. This road goes through Horqueta, Km 50, a cattle and lumber town with the usual petrol station, bank, bus station and inexpensive hotels and restaurants, most of which are either spread out along the motorway or clustered about the main plaza. Further on the road is very scenic. From Yby Yaú (69 km from Horqueta at the junction with Ruta 8, which turns south to Coronel Oviedo) the road continues to Pedro Juan Caballero.

Parque Nacional Cerro Corá
www.salvemoslos.com.py/pncc.htm.

Almost 50 km east of Yby Yaú, Ruta 5 continues through the pleasant Parque Nacional Cerro Corá, now much reduced in size to 5538 ha. To access the park from the main entrance, take the left-turning branch road (marked) some 6 km from Yby Yaú. Not far from the park's entrance is a small historical museum, a visitor centre, and monument to López and other national heroes. Although literally in the middle of nowhere, the site is constantly guarded as a matter of national pride. It has hills and cliffs (some with pre-Columbian caves and petroglyphs, which until recently were believed to be evidence that Vikings once visited the area), camping facilities, swimming and hiking trails. The rocky outcrops are spectacular and the warden is helpful and provides free guides. When you have walked up the road and seen the line of the country's former leaders' heads, turn right and go up the track passing a dirty-looking shack (straight on leads to a military base; access prohibited). The park's administration office (not a recommended entry point) is 5 km east of the main entrance at Km 180 back on Ruta 5.

Pedro Juan Caballero

functional frontier town; not a place to hang around

The border town of Pedro Juan Caballero (population 81,650) is separated from the Brazilian town of Ponta Porã by a road (called 'Dr Francia' on the Paraguayan side; on the Brazilian side it's known as either 'Rua Marechal Floreano' or 'Avenida Internacional'), which anyone can cross.

See below for immigration formalities. Ponta Porã is the more modern and prosperous of the two towns; everything costs less on the Paraguayan side. The enormous **Shopping China** ① *Ruta V y Av Internacional, T0336-274343, www. shoppingchina.com.py, daily 0800-1900*, is a vast emporium on the eastern suburbs of town, reputed to have the best shopping in the Americas (it has to be seen to be believed). The pristine **Maxi** ① *J M Estibarribia y Mcal López, T0336-274888, www.maxi.com.py*, is a large well-stocked supermarket with a **Mr Grill** restaurant in the centre. You can pay in guaraníes, reais or US dollars, at good exchange rates. **Arte Paraguaya** ① *Mcal López y Alberdi*, has a selection of crafts from all over the country.

In recent years the town has attracted a prominent criminal element (based not so much on smuggling as drugs) and care should be taken at all times.

Border with Brazil

Pedro Juan Caballero This crossing is a more relaxed one than that at Ciudad del Este, and much faster. (It can't get much easier than walking across a road.) For day crossings you do not need a stamp (but remember to return before the Paraguayan checkpoint closes at 2100 each night), but passports must be stamped if travelling beyond the border towns (ask if unsure whether your destination is considered beyond). If you fail to get a stamp when entering Paraguay, you will be fined US$45 when you try to leave. **Paraguayan immigration** ① *T0336-272195, Mon-Fri 0700-2100, Sat 0800-2100, Sun 1900-2100; take bus line 2 on the Paraguayan side, or any Brazilian city bus that goes to the Rodoviária, taxi US$7.50*, is in the customs building (Avenida Francia y Itororó) on the eastern outskirts of town near the gargantuan **Shopping China complex**. Then cross the bridge and report to the Brazilian federal police in Ponta Porã (closed Saturday/Sunday). The **Brazilian consulate** ① *Mariscal Estigarribia 250, T973-444915, Mon-Fri 0800-1300*, issues visas. Fees are payable only in guaraníes; take your passport and a photo, and go early to get your visa on the same day.

There are many *cambios* on the Paraguayan side, especially on Curupayty between Dr Francia and Mcal López. There are good rates for buying guaraníes or reais with US dollars or euros cash (better than inside Brazil), but traveller's cheques are usually impossible to change and there is only one ATM. Banks on the Brazilian side do not change cash or traveller's cheques but have a variety of ATMs.

Bella Vista There is another crossing to Brazil at Bella Vista on the Río Apá, 142 km northwest of Pedro Juan Caballero along Ruta 5 west and then turning right at the entrance to the road for Parque Nacional Cerro Corá; buses run from the Brazilian border town of Bela Vista to Jardim and on to Campo Grande, also to Pedro Juan Caballero. There is a Paraguayan immigration office at Bella Vista, but on the other side there no corresponding Brazilian *policia federal*. To cross here, get your Paraguayan exit stamp then report to the local Brazilian police who may give a temporary stamp, but you must later go to the *policia federal* in either Ponta Porã or Corumbá. Do not fail to get the proper stamp in one of these two towns or you will be fined and detained upon re-entering Paraguay.

North of Concepción Passage to Brazil from Concepción and points north is similar to passage to Bolivia from the same points, as the Río Paraguay is the border with Brazil for many kilometres before it reaches Bolivia. *Aquidabán* cargo boats (expensive) go north of Concepción to Vallemí, Fuerte Olimpo, and **Bahía Negra** and occasionally stop at intermediate points along the upper Río Paraguay, through the Pantanal de Nebileque (see Transport, page 99). This is also the route to Bolivia, but because of the time involved, it is important to get a pre-dated exit stamp at **Immigration** ⓘ *Registro Civil, Pdte Franco y Caballero, Concepción, T972-193143*, if you wish to leave Paraguay this way. Near Bahía Negra on the banks of the Río Negro, just over the border from Bolivia, is the 15,000-ha **Los Tres Gigantes** biological station, which has lodging. Contact **Guyra Paraguay** ⓘ *Asunción, T021-223567, www.guyra.org.py*, in advance for details. It can only be reached by boat (US$90 round trip, boat takes four people) and is a wonderful place to see Pantanal wildlife, including (with luck) jaguar and giant anteater. There is accommodation; full board can be arranged for roughly US$35 per person per day.

Listings Pedro Juan Caballero

Where to stay

$$$-$$ Eiruzú
Mcal López y Mcal Estigarribia, T0336-272435.
A/c, fridge and pool, starting to show its age but still good.

$$$-$$ Porã Palace
Alberdi 30 y Dr Francia, T0336-273021, www.porapalacehotel.com.
A/c, fridge, balcony, restaurant, pool, OK, rooms in upper floor have been refurbished and are nicer.

$ Victoria
Teniente Herrero y Alberdi, near bus station, T0336-272733.
Electric shower and a/c, cheaper with fan, family run, simple. Cheapest decent lodgings in town. Cash only.

Border with Brazil
Bahía Negra

$$ Tres Gigantes
In the reserve, T021-229097 (Asunción).
Rustic but peaceful, meals extra and must be confirmed ahead of time.

$ Hombre y Naturaleza
T982-898589.
Run by a recognized conservation group.

$ La Victoria
Av Principal, T982-469942.
Basic but the best of its class in town.

$$-$ Peppe's
Av Dr Francia y Alberdi. Daily for breakfast, lunch and dinner.
Overwhelming favourite in town, rave reviews. Wonderful beef and scallops, Paraguayan soups and other local dishes hard to find elsewhere.

There are many decent restaurants across the border in Ponta Porã along Av Brasil and Rua Paraguai. In particular, **Restaurante Nippon**, rumoured to be one of the best of its kind in Brazil, should not be missed for fans of Japanese food.

Bus To **Concepción**, as above. To **Asunción**, quickest route is via Yby Yaú, Santa Rosa and 25 de Diciembre, about 6 hrs. **La Santaniana** has nicest buses, *bus cama* US$17.50; *semicama* US$12; *común* US$10.50. Also **La Ovetense** and **Nasa-Golondrina** 2 a day on the quick route. To **Bella Vista**, Perpetuo Socorro 3 a day, US$8, 4 hrs. To **Campo Grande Amambay** 3 a day, US$21, 5 hrs, they stop at Policia Federal in Ponta Porã for entry stamp.

The Chaco

★ West of the Río Paraguay is the Chaco, a wild expanse of palm savannah and marshes (known as Humid, or Bajo Chaco, closest to the Río Paraguay) and dry scrub forest and farmland (known as Dry, or Alto Chaco, further northwest from the river). The Chaco is one of the last homelands of Paraguay's indigenous peoples, now numbering some 27,000 inhabitants. In recent years the region has suffered the highest deforestation rate anywhere on the continent, but birdlife and desert-dwelling wildlife are spectacular and abundant. Large cattle estancias dot the whole region, but otherwise agriculture has been developed mainly by German-speaking Mennonites from Russia, clustered around three unique communities in the Chaco Central. Through this vast, silent area the Trans-Chaco Highway (Ruta 9) runs to Bolivia. Most of the region is pristine, perfect for those who want to escape into the wilderness with minimal human contact and experience nature at its finest, have the funds to mount a lengthy trip, and know the risks involved in traversing the terrain. Although the government has made much of its interest in promoting tourism in the Chaco, it is also considerably lacking in communication networks, infrastructure and resources, so travellers should prepare accordingly.

Best for
Wilderness ▪ Wildlife

Finding your feet

The Paraguayan Chaco covers more than 24 million ha, but once away from the vicinity of Asunción, the average density is far less than one person to the square kilometre. A single major highway, the Ruta Trans-Chaco (Ruta 9), runs in an almost straight line northwest towards the Bolivian border, ostensibly forming part of the *corredor bi-oceánico*, connecting ports on the Pacific and Atlantic oceans, although it has yet to live up to its expectations.

The elevation rises very gradually from 50 m opposite Asunción to 450 m on the Bolivian border. Paving of the Trans-Chaco to the Bolivian border (ending at the military outpost of Fortín Sargento Rodríguez) was completed in 2007, but in spite of being graded twice a year, several paved sections are showing signs of wear and tear, with repairs to potholes few and far between. Sand berms also form at will in some sections and must be avoided. During the rainy season the route is flooded and all but impassable.

However, most travellers access Bolivia not by passing through Sargento Rodríguez, but rather through another military base to the southwest, Infante Rivarola, which is gained by turning left from the Ruta Trans-Chaco in Estancia La Patria onto a hard-packed road. (Note that, as a military base, it does not provide exit stamps; if you are proceeding on to Bolivia you will need to return to Mariscal Estigarribia to get one.)

Although road conditions in the Chaco are much improved in parts, motorists and even travellers going by bus should carry extra food and especially water; climatic conditions are harsh and there is little traffic in case of a breakdown.

Getting around

Most bus companies now have some air-conditioned buses on their Chaco routes (a great asset December-March), but enquire in advance as otherwise the ride is stiflingly hot. There is very little local public transport between the main Mennonite towns (and distances between the communities are not short), so you must use the buses heading to or from Asunción to travel between the few of them that have service as well as Mariscal Estigarribia. At present, only Loma Plata, Neuland and Filadelfia are served; neither Pozo Colorado to the south nor any of the military posts or estancias to the north have bus services.

Tours

Many agencies in Asunción offer Chaco tours. Note that some are just a visit to **Rancho Buffalo Bill** and do not provide a good overview of attractions. **Hans Fast** in Loma Plata, *T0492-252422, fast@telesurf.com.py* and **Harry Epp** in Neuland also run tours to national parks. In Loma Plata ask around for bicycle hire to explore nearby villages. For more complete tailor-made tours, contact **Guyra Paraguay** (www.guyra.org. py). This birding organization does not offer tours of the Chaco, but can make excellent referrals to those operators that meet its high standards.

Always examine in detail a tour operator's claims to expertise in the Chaco.

Going it alone

No private expedition should leave the Ruta Trans-Chaco without plentiful supplies of water, food and fuel, nor should anyone venture onto the dirt roads alone. This is a major smuggling route from Bolivia, and it is unwise to stop for anyone at night. There are service stations at regular intervals along the highway in the Bajo and Chaco Central, but beyond Mariscal Estigarribia there is one stop for diesel only and no regular petrol at all until Villamontes in Bolivia – a long drive.

When to go

Winter temperatures are warm by day, cooler by night, but summer heat and mosquitoes can make it very unpleasant (pyrethrum coils, *espirales*, are sold everywhere).

Tip...

Any unusual insect bites should be examined immediately, as Chagas disease is endemic in the Chaco.

Tourist information

Consejo Regional de Turismo Chaco Central (CONRETUR) coordinates tourism development of the three cooperatives and the private sector. **Fundación para el Desarrollo Sustentable del Chaco**, *Deportivo 935 y Algarrobo, Loma Plata, T0492-252235, fdschaco@telesurf.com.py*, operates conservation projects in the area and has useful information but does not offer tours. See also under individual towns for local tourist offices.

Reserva de la Biosfera del Chaco
pristine nature reserve with big mammals, but hard to access

This is one of the crown jewels of Paraguay's national park system, albeit one without infrastructure and nearly impossible to visit.

Guyra Paraguay ① *Gaetano Martino 215 y Tte Ross, T021-223567, www.guyra.org.py, Mon-Fri 0800-1700*, which currently co-manages the national parks in this region, is possibly the best option for arranging a tour (see National parks, page 60 and Tours, page 106). Note that any expedition to the reserve will be a very costly undertaking and must be cleared with government authorities well ahead of time.

The 4.7 million-ha biosphere reserve, straddling the Chaco and Pantanal ecosystems is a UNESCO Man and Biosphere Reserve and includes six protected areas. The **Parque Nacional Defensores del Chaco** ① *www.salvemoslos.com.py/pdchaco.htm*, at 780,000 ha, is considered a pristine environment and the gateway to the seventh-largest ecosystem in Latin America and is the largest entity in the biosphere. It is some 220 km from Filadelfia and has a biological station, but only one staffed ranger station at Madrejón in the southeastern corner with very limited facilities: some water, restricted electricity and a small shop for truckers. There are currently no other ranger stations in operation. **Parque Nacional Teniente Agripino Enciso** ① *www.salvemoslos.com.py/pntae.htm*, is 20 km from La Patria. Nasa minibuses run from Filadelfia to Teniente Enciso via Mariscal Estigarribia and La Patria. The reserve also contains **Médanos del Chaco** ① *www.salvemoslos.com.py/pnmc.htm*, and **Río Negro** ① *www.salvemoslos.com.py/pnrn.htm*, national parks; the **Cerro Chovoreca natural monument**; and the **Cerro Cabrera Timané Reserve**, which at 502,250 ha is the second-largest reserve. All are north of the Trans-Chaco, mostly along the Bolivian border; the Cerro Chovoreca literally forms part of it. Most of Paraguay's few remaining jaguars are found here. Puma, tapir and peccary also inhabit the area, as well as *taguá* (an endemic peccary) and a short-haired guanaco. The best time to see them is around waterholes at nightfall in the dry season, but with great patience. **Cerro León** (highest peak 600 m) is one of the only hilly areas of the Chaco. It is located within PN Defensores del Chaco and in 2015 was under threat on a variety of fronts, including the extraction of stone for road building.

The Trans-Chaco Highway 1: to Loma Plata
hundreds of kilometres with no major towns en route; a real adventure

To reach the Ruta Trans-Chaco, leave Asunción behind and cross the Río Paraguay to **Villa Hayes** on Ruta 9. Birdlife is immediately more abundant and easily visible in the palm savannah, but other wildlife is usually only seen at night, and otherwise occurs mostly as road kill.

After the Copetrol station in Villa Hayes, the next service station is not until you reach at Km 130. **Pirahú**, Km 252, has a service station and is a good place to stop for a meal; it has air-conditioning, delicious *empanadas* and fruit salad. The owner

BACKGROUND

The Chaco

The **Bajo Chaco** begins on the riverbank just west of Asunción across the Río Paraguay. It is a picturesque landscape of palm savannah, much of which is seasonally inundated because of the impenetrable clay beneath the surface, although there are temporary 'islands' of higher ground with forest vegetation. Cattle ranching on huge, isolated estancias is the prevailing economic activity. Except in an emergency, it is not advisable to enter an estancia unless you have prior permission from the owner.

In the **Chaco Central**, the natural vegetation becomes dry scrub forest, with a mixture of hardwoods and cactus. The *palo borracho* (bottle tree) with its pear-shaped, water-conserving trunk, the *palo santo*, with its green wood and beautiful scent, and the tannin-rich *quebracho* (literally meaning axe-breaker) are the most noteworthy native species. This is the best area in Paraguay to see large mammals (always with a guide who knows the area well as markers are non-existent), especially once away from the central Chaco Mennonite colonies.

The **Alto Chaco** is characterized by low dense thorn and scrub forest which has created an impenetrable barricade of spikes and spiny branches resistant to heat and drought and which are very tough on tyres. Towards Bolivia cacti become more prevalent as rainfall decreases. There are a few estancias in the southern part, but beyond Mariscal Estigarribia there are only occasional military checkpoints. Summer temperatures often exceed 45°C.

For all of the Chaco's abundant wildlife and protected areas, the traveller should consider the role that deforestation plays in the gradual but very real destruction of this unique environment. According to reports from **Guyra Paraguay** (see below), more than half a million hectares were deforested throughout the entire Gran Chaco (which includes portions of Argentina and Bolivia as well as more than half of Paraguay's territory) during 2013 alone, equivalent to a rate of 1376 ha per day. The average rate of continuous forest loss in the region was a staggering 57.33 ha per hour, that's one hectare per minute. Of the total deforestation, Paraguay accounted for by far the largest amount, with 236,869 ha cleared.

of the Ka-Í parador owns an old-fashioned carbon manufacturing site 2 km before Pirahú. Ask for him if you are interested in visiting the site. At Km 271 is **Pozo Colorado** and the turning east onto Ruta 5 for Concepción (see page 95). There are two restaurants, a basic hotel ($ with fan, cheaper without), supermarket, hospital, two service stations and a military post. The **Touring y Automóvil Club Paraguayo** ⓘ *T981-939611, www.tacpy.com.py*, provides a breakdown and recovery service from Pozo Colorado. At this point, the tidy Mennonite homesteads, with flower gardens and citrus orchards, begin to appear. At Km 282, 14 km northwest of Pozo Colorado, is **Rancho Buffalo Bill** (Asunción number T021-298381), one of the most pleasant places to stop off or eat, beside a small lake. The estancia has limited but good accommodation ($$-$); ask at the restaurant. Horse riding, nature walks and camping are good options here. At Km 320 is **Río Verde**, with fuel, police station and restaurant. The next good place to stay or eat along the Trans-Chaco is **Cruce de los Pioneros**, at Km 415, where there is accommodation ($$-$ **Los Pioneros**, T0491-432170, hot shower, a/c), a limited supermarket, vehicle repair shop and fuel. A paved road runs from **Cruce Boquerón**, just northwest of Cruce de los Pioneros, to **Loma Plata**. In mid-September the country's biggest motorsport event, the **Trans-Chaco Rally** (www.rally.com.py), is held.

Listings The Trans-Chaco Highway

Where to stay

Villa Hayes

$$$ pp Estancia Golondrina
José Domingo Ocampo, Km 235, San Luis, Asunción office, Pastor Ibáñez 2275 casi Av Artigas, T021-282704 (weekdays only), www.estanciagolondrina.com.
Take the unpaved road to the right, 15 km to the ranch. A good place for combining rural and ecotourism. The ranch has extensive agricultural land as well as 12,000 ha of protected virgin forest (Reserva Ypetí) and abundant wildlife. There are trails for walking or horse riding, boat trips on the river, picturesque accommodation (a/c, private bathroom, very comfortable) overlooking the river. Price includes all meals, activities and transportation from the main road.

Mennonite communities
well-organized but isolated towns in an otherwise hostile region

The Chaco Central has been settled by Mennonites, Anabaptists of German extraction who began arriving in the late 1920s. There are three administratively distinct but adjacent colonies: **Menno** (from Russia via Canada, the oldest and largest, settled in 1927); **Fernheim** (directly from Russia, the second largest, founded in 1930); and **Neuland** (the last group to arrive, from Ukraine in 1947).

The last group to arrive came in 1983 and settled in **Colonia Manitoba**, east of Concepción. Among themselves, most Mennonites still speak 'plattdeutsch' ('Low' German), but they readily speak and understand 'hochdeutsch' ('High German'), which is the language of instruction in their schools. Increasingly, younger Mennonites speak Spanish and some English. Although seemingly aloof, the people are friendly and willing to talk about their history and culture. Altogether in the Chaco Boreal there are about 70 small settlements with a population of about 18,000 Mennonites (out of some 30,000 throughout the country) and 20,000 *indígenas* from eight distinct groups (who traditionally have occupied the lowest rung on the socio-economic ladder).

In spite of early failures and the difficulty of adjusting to the region's intense heat and utter lack of infrastructure, the Mennonites have been almost uniformly successful throughout Paraguay, but in the Chaco in particular they have created a remarkable oasis of regimented prosperity in this harsh hinterland. Their hotels and restaurants are impeccably clean, services are very efficient, large modern supermarkets are well stocked with excellent dairy products and all other goods, local and imported. Each colony has its own interesting museum. All services, except for hotels, a few restaurants and one gas station in Filadelfia, close on Saturday afternoon and Sunday. The main towns are all very spread out and have no public transport except for a few expensive taxis in Filadelfia; most residents use their private vehicles. Walking around in the dust and extreme heat can be tiring. Transport between the three main towns is also limited.

Filadelfia

Also known as **Fernheim Colony**, Filadelfia (population 11,742), 466 km from Asunción, is the largest town of the region, with about 50% of its inhabitants Mennonites. The **Museo Jakob Unger** ⓘ *Hindenburg y Unruh, T0491-32151, www.faunaparaguay.com/jakobunger.html, Mon-Fri 0700-1130 and 1400-1700, US$1 including video*, provides a glimpse of pioneer life in the Chaco, as well as exhibiting artefacts of the indigenous peoples of the region. The manager of the **Hotel Florida** will open the museum upon request. Next to the museum is **Plaza de los Recuerdos**, a good place to see the *samu'u* or *palo borracho* (bottle tree). A bookstore-cum-craft shop, **Librería El Mensajero** ⓘ *next to Hotel Florida, Av Hindenburg y Trébol, T0491-91354*, is run by Sra Penner who is very helpful and informative. There is an enormous dairy on the outskirts of town; informal tours can be arranged.

Apart from the website, www.filadelfiaparaguay.com, there is no tourist infrastructure in Filadelfia. General information may be obtained from the co-op office. Services in town include ATMs, banks, internet and phone office.

Loma Plata

The centre of Menno Colony, Loma Plata (population 4118) is 15 km east of Filadelfia. Although smaller than Filadelfia, it has more to offer the visitor, but few transport services. It has a good museum, **Museo de la Colonia Menno** ⓘ *Av Central, Mon-Fri 0700-1130, 1400-1800, Sat 0700-1130, US$1.85*, tracing the settlement's history through photographs and artefacts. The **Balneario Oasis swimming complex** ⓘ *Nord Grenze, 700 m past airport north of Loma Plata, T0492-52704, US$2, Sep-Apr 1500-2100, except Sun and holidays, 1100-2100*, is a welcome break from the summer heat and has three pools with slides and snack bar. The **tourist office** ⓘ *contact Walter Ratzlaff, next to the Chortitzer Komitee Co-op on Av Central, T0492-52301, turismo@chortitzer.com.py, Mon-Fri 0700-1130, 1400-1800, Sat 0700-1300*, is very helpful. Services in town include banks, ATMs, internet and telephone office.

Wetlands around Loma Plata To the southeast of Loma Plata is the Riacho Yacaré Sur watershed, with many saltwater lagoons, generally referred to as *laguna salada*. This is a wonderful place to see waterbirds such as Chilean flamingos, swans, spoonbills and migratory shorebirds from the Arctic. There are extensive walks though the eerily beautiful landscape.

Laguna Capitán, a 22-ha recreation reserve, 30 km from town, has several small lagoons, a swimming lake, basic bunk bed accommodation ($, shared bath), kitchen facilities, meals on request, camping. Make reservations directly at T983-344463, English and German spoken (also helpful for tour organizing), or through the Cooperative information office in Loma Plata. There is no public transport. Taxi US$30 one-way; full-day tour combining Laguna Capitán with a visit to the Cooperative's installations and museum, US$85 per group plus transport. Guides are required for visits.

Laguna Chaco Lodge ⓘ *70 km from town, T0492-252235*, a 2500-ha private reserve, is a Ramsar wetland site (no accommodation). Chaco Lodge is a saltwater lake, the largest of the water bodies in the lake system of the Central Chaco, surrounded by lush vegetation. The site is one of the few relatively undisturbed natural areas in the Chaco, with an impressive biodiversity including the endangered Chacoan peccary and the Brazilian tapir. Chaco Lodge is entirely devoted to conservation and small-scale ecotourism, and hunting and cattle ranching pressures from the surrounding area are very limited.

The lovely **Laguna Flamenco** is the main body of water surrounded by dry forest. Large numbers of Chilean flamingos and other waterbirds may be seen here. **Campo María** ⓘ *105 km from Filadelfia, www.chortitzer.com.py, US$2.50*, a 4500-ha reserve owned by the Chortitzer Komitee, also has a large lake and can be visited on a tour.

A visit to the **Indigenous Foundation for Agricultural and Livestock Development** (**FIDA**) ⓘ *30 km from Neuland, Filadelfia and Loma Plata, T0491-432321, www.ascim.org*, is worth a visit as well. Located within **Yalve Sanga**, a collective of 1762 indigenous inhabitants organized into 11 agricultural villages. The community has its own legal capacity and is the legal owner of 6000 ha of property. Yalve Sanga is the first indigenous version of the Mennonite cooperative colonies and provides an interesting insight into the lives of the tribal communities. Limited handicrafts are sold in the Yalve Sanga supermarket (there's a better selection in Neuland).

Neuland

Neuland (population 4217), also known as Neu-Halbstadt, is 381 km northwest of Asunción and 46 km southwest of Filadelfia. A well-organized town, it is the centre of the High Chaco's limited tourism infrastructure There is a small **Museo Histórico de la Asociación Colonia Neuland** ⓘ *Av 1 de Febrero, T0493-240201*, with objects brought by the first Mennonites from Russia, set in the building of the first primary school of the area. There's also **Neuland Beach Park** ⓘ *US$1.75, pool, snack bar with a/c*, and **Parque la Amistad**, 500 m past the pool, which consists of 35 ha of natural vegetation where paths have been cleared for nature walks. Most spectacular are the wild orchids (September-October), cacti and birdlife. Enrique (Heinz) Weibe (T971-701634, hwiebe@neuland.com.py) is the official guide of the Neuland colony; also ask for Harry Epp who you can contact through Neuland Co-op office

(i) *T0493-240201, www.neuland.com.py, Mon-Fri 0700-1130 and 1400-1800, Sat 0700-1130*. He is very knowledgeable about the flora and fauna and is an informative and entertaining guide. He also gives tours of Neuland in a horse-drawn carriage. Phone booths and post office are in centre of town next to the supermarket.

Fortín Boquerón, 25 km from Neuland, was the site of the decisive battle of Chaco War (September 1932) and includes a memorial, a small well-presented museum and walks around the remainder of the trenches. **Campamento Aurora Chaqueña**, a park 15 km from town on the way to Fortín Boquerón, has simple accommodation with fan ($, take your own food and water). **Parque Valle Natural**, 10 km from Neuland on the way to Filadelfia, is an *espartillar*, a dry riverbed with natural brush around it and a few larger trees. Camping is possible although there is only a small covered area. All three sites are easily reached from Neuland as part of a package tour.

Listings Mennonite communities

Tourist information

If in Asunción, a good source of information on the Mennonite colonies throughout all of Paraguay is the **Asociación de Colonias Mennonitas del Paraguay** *(Colombia y Estados Unidos, T021-226059, www.acomepa.org)* which also has offices in Filadelfia and Loma Plata. See also page 107.

Where to stay

Filadelfia

$$-$ Golondrina-Avenida
Av Hindenburg 635-S at entrance to town, T0491-433111, www.hotel golondrina.com.
Modern, 4 types of room with breakfast, a/c, fridge in the best (cheapest with fan, shared bath, no breakfast), restaurant.

$$-$ Golondrina-Centro
Industrial 194-E, T0491-432218, www. hotelgolondrina.com/?Centro.
Modern, spacious common areas with game room. Spanish and German spoken.

$ Florida
Av Hindenburg 165-S opposite park, T0491-432151, http://hotelfloridachaco. com. Fridge, a/c, breakfast, cheaper in basic annex with shared bath, fan and without breakfast.
Pool (US$1.50 per hr for non-guests), restaurant ($) for buffet and à la carte.

There is a **Touring y Automóvil Club Paraguayo** hotel at Transchaco Km 443, www.tacpy.com.py.

Loma Plata

$$-$ Loma Plata Inn
Eligio Ayala y Manuel Gondra, T0492-252166, www.lomaplata innhotel.com.
Near southern roundabout and Nasa bus office, with restaurant.

$$-$ Mora
Sandstrasse 803, T0492-252255.
With breakfast, a/c, Wi-Fi, new wing has spacious rooms with fridge, nice grounds, family run, good value, good breakfast, basic meals on request. Recommended.

$$-$ Pensión Loma Plata
J B Reimer 1805, T0492-252829.
A/c, breakfast, comfortable rooms,
homely atmosphere, very helpful, good
value. Includes breakfast, other meals
on request.

Neuland

$$-$ Hotel Boquerón
*Av 1 de Febrero opposite the Cooperative,
T0493-240306, www.neuland.com.py/
en/services/hotel-restaurant-boqueron.*
With breakfast, a/c, cheaper in older
wing without TV, restaurant.

$ Parador
*Av 1 de Febrero y C Talleres,
T0493-240567.*
With breakfast, a/c, cheaper with fan
and shared bath, restaurant.

Restaurants

Filadelfia

$ El Girasol
*Unruh 126-E y Hindenburg, T0491-
320780. Mon-Sat 1100-1400, 1800-2300,
Sun 1100-1400.*
Good buffet and *rodizio*, cheaper
without the meat.

Loma Plata

$$ Chaco's Grill
Av Dr Manuel Gondra, T0492-252166.
Buffet, *rodizio*, very good, patio,
live music.

$ Norteño
3 Palmas 990, T0492-252447.
Good, simple, lunch till 1400 then open
for dinner.

$ Pizzería San Marino
Av Central y Dr Gondra. Daily 1800-2300.
Pizza and German dishes.

$ Unión
*Av Central, north of roundabout, halfway
to airport. Daily 0800-1300, 1700-2200.*
Good standard food.

Transport

Filadelfia
Bus From **Asunción**, Nasa-Golondrina,
3 daily except Sat, US$12; also **Stel
Turismo**, 1 overnight; 6 hrs. To **Loma
Plata**, Nasa-Golondrina 0800 going to
Asunción, 0600 and 1900 coming from
Asunción, 1 hr, US$3.50. To **Neuland**,
local service Mon-Fri 1130 and 1800, 1 hr,
US$3.50. Also **Stel Turismo** at 1900 and
Nasa-Golondrina at 2130, both coming
from Asunción. To **Mariscal Estigarribia**,
Nasa at 0500 Mon and Fri, continuing to
La Patria and Parque Nacional Teniente
Enciso (see page 108), 5-6 hrs, US$12,
returns around 1300 same day (confirm
all details in advance).

Loma Plata
Bus **Asunción**, Nasa-Golondrina, daily
0600, 7-8 hrs, US$12. To **Filadelfia**, Mon-
Fri 1300, Sat 1100, Sun 1200, daily 2130,
all continuing to Asunción.

Neuland
Bus To **Asunción**, Stel Turismo at
1900 (1230 on Sat), via Filadelfia, 7-8 hrs,
US$12. Local service to **Filadelfia**, Mon-
Fri 0500, 1230.

Mariscal Estigarribia

At 525 km from Asunción, the few amenities in Mariscal Estigarribia (population 14,035) are spread out over 4 km along the Trans-Chaco Highway: three service stations, a couple of small supermarkets (La Llave del Chaco is recommended), two mediocre hotels, and one remarkably excellent restaurant. There are no banks, but the Shell station changes US dollars cash. Copaco phone office is one street back from the highway. The immigration office (supposedly 24 hours, but often closed in the small hours, so best to pick up any pre-dated exit steps needed for Bolivia in Asunción or Concepción, as those further north are also often closed) is at the southeast end of town near the Shell station. All buses stop at the terminal (Parador Arami), at the northwest end of town, where travellers entering from Bolivia are subject to thorough searches for drugs. The people are friendly and helpful.

Border with Bolivia

There are no reliable services of any kind beyond Mariscal Estigarribia. At La Patria, 125 km northwest, the road divides: 128 km west to Infante Rivarola continuing to Villamontes (Bolivia), with Bolivian immigration and customs at Ibibobo; or 128 km northwest to General Eugenio A Garay continuing to Boyuibe (Bolivia). This route is not used by public transport. You can traverse it in a private vehicle but cannot cross the border into Bolivia without prior permission and government-authorized papers as there are no facilities for processing exit stamps. Immigration posts are at Mariscal Estigarribia and Ibibobo (the latter often closed, so always best to use the former). For the southwestern route, there are customs posts at either side of the actual border in addition to the main customs offices in Mariscal Estigarribia and Villamontes.

In Bolivia, from Villamontes, a paved road runs north to Santa Cruz and south to Yacuiba on the Argentine border. Take small-denomination dollar notes as it is impossible to buy bolivianos before reaching Bolivia. (If entering Paraguay from Bolivia, only *casas de cambio* in Santa Cruz or Puerto Suárez – none in Camiri or Boyuibe – have guaraníes.)

Listings Mariscal Estigarribia to Bolivia

Where to stay

$ Parador Arami
Northwest end of town and far from everything, also known as 'la terminal', T0494-247277.
Functional rooms, a/c, meals on request, agents for Stel Turismo and Nasa buses.

Restaurants

$$ Italiano
Southwest end of town behind Shell station, T0494-247231.
Excellent, top quality meat, large portions, an unexpected treat. Italian owner is friendly and helpful, open for lunch and dinner.

Transport

Bus From **Filadelfia**, Nasa-Golondrina 1100 daily; **Asunción**, Nasa-Golondrina, daily 1430, and **Pycasu** 3 daily, US$12; **Stel**, 2 a day, US$13.75, 7-8 hrs. Buses from Asunción pass through town around 0300-0400 en route to Bolivia: **Yaciretá** on Tue, Thu, Sat, Sun (agent at Barcos y Rodados petrol station, T0494-247320); **Stel Turismo** daily (agent at Parador Arami, T0494-247230). You can book and purchase seats in advance but beware overcharging, the fare from Mariscal Estigarribia should be about US$10 less than from Asunción.

Background
Paraguay

History

Pre-independence history

Since 1516 European seafarers had visited the Río de la Plata, first Juan de Solís, then Sebastian Cabot and his rival Diego García in 1527. An expedition led by Pedro de Mendoza founded Buenos Aires in 1536, but it was abandoned in 1541. Mendoza sent Juan de Ayolas up the Río Paraná to reach Peru from the east. It is not known for certain what happened to Ayolas, but his lieutenant Domingo Martínez de Irala founded Asunción on the Río Paraguay in 1537. This was the base from which the Spaniards relaunched their conquest of the Río de la Plata and Buenos Aires was refounded in 1580.

The Jesuits established themselves in Paraguay as early as 1588 with the permission of the Spanish king, Philip II. Starting in 1610, they established 30 missions, or *reducciones*. One of the main objectives of the Jesuits' presence in what is now Paraguay was the protection of the local peoples against the abuses of the colonial *encomienda* system of forced labour, which reduced them to a condition of virtual slavery; at the same time, the Jesuits hoped that a non-antagonistic approach to evangelizing the Guaraní and other peoples would bring them into the Catholic Church and enable them to adjust to a more sedentary form of life. Previously confined to the area around Asunción and a few towns to the southeast, with the granting of the frontier zone of Paraguay to the Jesuits in 1609 by the Spanish Crown, they immediately moved into the Río de la Plata basin, where they created some 30 *reducciones*, in the process spreading further afield to Argentina, Bolivia, Brazil and Uruguay. The Jesuit missions were by all accounts the most successful group of missions established in Spanish America, and at their height in the early 1730s had a population of as many as 140,000 Guaraní. These so-called 'Jesuit Republics' or the 'Jesuit Theocracy' were the subject of contemporary literature (Voltaire's *Candide*), as well as modern literature and film (Scorsese's *The Mission*).

In the 1620s and 1630s, slave raiders from Sao Paulo (*bandeirantes*) forced the Jesuits to relocate a number of missions, until they finally organized a Guaraní militia and defeated the raiders in 1641. The Guaraní militia became a useful tool to the Spanish government in the remote and essentially lawless region, but was also a source of tension with local settlers. In 1750, Spain and Portugal signed the Treaty of Madrid to establish the boundaries between Spanish and Portuguese territory in South America. Portugal was to receive seven missions located east of the Río Uruguay, and the Guaraní were to relocate. Instead, they revolted, leading to the so-called Guaraní War, one of few first pre-Independence uprisings by indigenous peoples in the continent to experience any degree of success. At the same time, the missions prospered, and became major – or in some cases, even the most dominant – participants in the regional economy, selling yerba mate, cattle hides, cotton, and other products throughout the region. This arrangement stayed in place until the Jesuits were expelled from all Spanish territories in 1767 by royal decree.

BACKGROUND
The Jesuits

Between 1610, when they built their first *reducción* (mission) in present-day Paraguay, and 1767, when they were expelled from Spanish America, the Jesuits founded some 30 missions around the upper reaches of the rivers Paraná, Paraguay and Uruguay. In 1627, the northern missions around Guaíra were attacked by slave hunters (*bandeirantes*) from São Paulo, forcing the inhabitants to flee southwards. Some 10,000 converts, led by their priests, floated 700 rafts down the Río Parapanema into the Paraná, only to find their route blocked by the Guaíra Falls. Pushing on for eight days through dense forest, they built new boats below the falls and continued their journey to reestablish their missions 725 km from their original homes. Efficiently organized and strictly laid out, the missions prospered, growing indigenous and European crops and herding cattle. Their success and economic power attracted many enemies, from the Spanish Crown to local landowners. When, in 1750, Spain and Portugal settled their South American border dispute, seven missions were placed under Portuguese control. This the Jesuits resisted with arms, fuelling further the suspicion of the order's excessive power. Under highest secrecy, King Carlos III sent instructions to South America in 1767 to expel the Jesuits. 2000 were shipped to Europe, their property was auctioned and their schools and colleges were taken over by the Franciscans and Dominicans. By the early 19th century, many of the missions had fallen into disrepair. Outside of Bolivia's Jesuit missions of the Chiquitania (where seven have been restored to their original glory) only four missions in the region show signs of their former splendour: San Ignacio Miní in Argentina; Jesús de Tavarangue and La Santísima Trinidad in Paraguay; and São Miguel in Brazil.

Towards independence

Disturbances in neighbouring Buenos Aires in 1810-1816, which led to independence from Spain, enabled Creole leaders in Asunción to throw off the rule of Buenos Aires as well as Madrid. The new republic was, however, subject to pressure from both Argentina, which blocked Paraguayan trade on the Río de la Plata, and Brazil. Following independence Paraguay was ruled by a series of dictators, the first of whom, Dr Gaspar Rodríguez de Francia (1814-1840), known as 'El Supremo', imposed a policy of isolation and self-sufficiency. The opening of the Río de la Plata after the fall of the Argentine dictator Rosas enabled de Francia's successor, Carlos Antonio López (1840-1862) to import modern technology: in 1856 a railway line between Asunción and Villarrica was begun; an iron foundry and telegraph system were also developed. Carlos López was succeeded by his son, Francisco Solano López (López II), who saw himself as the Napoleon of South America. Believing Paraguay to be threatened by Brazil and Argentina, Solano López declared war on Brazil in 1865. When Argentina refused permission to send troops through Misiones to attack Brazil, López declared war on Argentina. With Uruguay supporting Brazil and Argentina, the ensuing War of the Triple Alliance was disastrous for the Paraguayan forces, who held on against overwhelming odds until the death of López at the Battle of Cerro Corá on 1 March 1870. Of a pre-war population of 400,000, only 220,000 survived the war, 28,000 of them males, mostly either very young or very old. In the peace settlement Paraguay lost territory to Brazil and Argentina, although rivalry between these neighbours prevented a worse fate.

After the war, Paraguay experienced political instability as civilian factions competed for power, often appealing to the army officers for support. Although there were few policy differences between the two political parties (the National Republican Association, known as Colorados from its red banner, and the Liberal party, who adopted the colour blue), rivalry was intense. Elections were held regularly, but whichever party was in government invariably intervened to fix the result and the opposition rarely participated.

The Chaco War

While Paraguayan leaders were absorbed with domestic disputes, Bolivia began occupying disputed parts of the Chaco in an attempt to gain access to the sea via the Río Paraguay. Although Bolivian moves started in the late 19th century, the dispute was given new intensity by the discovery of oil in the 1920s. In the four-year Chaco War (1932-1935) 56,000 Bolivians and 36,000 Paraguayans were killed. Despite general expectations, outnumbered Paraguayan troops under Mariscal José Félix Estigarribia pushed the Bolivian army out of most of the Chaco.

Victory in war only increased dissatisfaction in the army with the policies of pre-war governments. In February 1936 nationalist officers seized power and appointed the war hero, Colonel Rafael Franco as President. Although Franco was overthrown in a counter-coup in 1937, the so-called 'February Revolution' began major changes in Paraguay including the first serious attempt at land reform and legal recognition of the small labour movement. Between 1939 and 1954 Paraguayan politics were even more turbulent, as rival civilian factions and army officers vied for power. In 1946 civil war shook the country as army units based in Concepción fought to overthrow President Morínigo.

The Stroessner years

A military coup in May 1954 led to General Alfredo Stroessner becoming president. Stroessner retained power for 34 years, the most durable dictator in Paraguayan history and one of the longest in power in Latin America. His rule was based on control over the army and the Colorado party, both of which were purged of opponents. While a network of spies informed on dissidents, party membership was made compulsory for most official posts including teachers and doctors. In fraudulent elections Stroessner was re-elected eight times. Paraguay, and in particular the outlaw town of Puerto Presidente Stroessner (now Ciudad del Este), became a centre for smuggling, gambling and drug-running, much of it controlled by Stroessner's supporters. Meanwhile the government spent large amounts of money on transportation and infrastructure projects, including the giant hydroelectric dam at Itaipú. Although these projects brought employment, the completion of Itaipú in 1982 coincided with recession in Brazil and Argentina on whose economies Paraguay was heavily dependent. Meanwhile rivalry intensified within the regime over the succession, with Stroessner favouring his son, Gustavo. Opposition focussed around General Andrés Rodríguez, who was married to Stroessner's daughter. When Stroessner tried to force Rodríguez to retire, troops loyal to Rodríguez overthrew the 75-year-old Stroessner, who left to live in Brazil where he died in exile in 2006.

Liberalization

Rodríguez, who became provisional president, easily won multi-party elections in May 1989. The commitment to greater democracy permitted opponents who had previously boycotted, or been banned from elections, to gain an unprecedented number of seats in the legislative elections of the same date. Despite considerable scepticism over General Rodríguez's intentions, political liberalization became a reality. The presidential and congressional elections that he promised were held on 9 May 1993. The presidency was won by Juan Carlos Wasmosy of the Colorado Party and Domingo Laíno of the Authentic Radical Liberal Party came second.

The government's commitment to market reforms, privatization and economic integration with Argentina and Brazil within Mercosur inspired protests from all quarters. 1994 saw the first general strike in 35 years. There were also demands for land reform and increased social services. A worsening of relations between the military and the legislature led to a critical few days in April 1996. Army commander General Lino Oviedo was dismissed for threatening a coup; Wasmosy offered him the defence ministry but then withdrew the offer after massive public protest. Oviedo was later arrested on charges of insurrection, but to the dismay of the Colorado leadership, he was chosen as the party's candidate for the May 1998 presidential elections. This intensified the feud between Oviedo and Wasmosy, who eventually succeeded in having Oviedo jailed by a military tribunal for 10 years for the 1996 coup attempt. A compromise ticket of Raúl Cubas Grau (Oviedo's former running mate) and Luis María Argaña (Colorado party president and opponent of Wasmosy) won the election. Within a week of taking office in August 1998, Cubas released Oviedo from prison, despite a Supreme Court ruling that Oviedo should serve out his sentence. Matters came to a head when Vice President Argaña was shot in March 1999, just before the Senate was to vote on impeachment of Cubas. Intense diplomatic efforts, led by Paraguay's Mercosur partners, resulted in Cubas' resignation on 29 March. He was replaced by Luis González Macchi, the president of Congress. Cubas went into exile in Brazil, and Oviedo in Argentina, from where he escaped in December 1999. His military supporters staged an unsuccessful coup in May 2000 and the following month Oviedo was arrested in Brazil. The González Macchi administration, meanwhile, was facing economic recession, strikes and social discontent. The economic downturn and its repercussions worsened through 2002 as a result of Argentina's financial crisis. In February 2003, González Macchi himself was discredited by allegations of the misuse of state funds, fraud and the torture of left-wing militants (he was imprisoned for illegal enrichment in 2006). Nevertheless, in subsequent elections in April 2003, voters backed the Colorado Party and its candidate, Nicanor Duarte Frutos.

The end of Colorado rule

That nothing really changed under Duarte, certainly no improvement in the living conditions of the poor majority despite record incomes from soya exports, was one of the main causes of the demise of the Colorado presidency. In 2006, Fernando Lugo, the former bishop of San Pedro diocese, left the priesthood to enter politics and soon emerged as an independent, left-leaning leader of those seeking change. He contested the April 2008 elections as a member of the coalition Patriotic Alliance for Change party, with land reform and renegotiation of the treaty with Brazil defining sales of electricity from Itaipú as principal policies. Lugo easily defeated Colorado candidate Blanca Ovelar and Lino Oviedo (who had been released from prison in 2007), but had no political party to back him in congress. The Colorado party had won most seats in both houses. Lugo's inauguration was the first in Paraguay's history in which a ruling party peacefully ceded power to an elected president from an opposition party. Early in 2009, political developments were overshadowed by claims that Lugo had fathered sons with three different women. He did acknowledge one, but the allegations lost him much prestige. He also had to undergo treatment for cancer in 2010. Meanwhile, the activities of a small insurgent group, **Ejército del Pueblo Paraguayo** (EPP), such as kidnapping, forced Lugo to suspend constitutional rights in parts of the country in 2010. On the plus side, the economy in 2010 grew at an unprecedented rate, by some 15% according to the Central Bank, thanks to high prices and demand for Paraguay's main commodities, soya, beef and grains. After reduced growth in 2011 and again in 2012, the economy was almost back at 2010 levels of growth in 2013. Unlike some, the vast majority of Paraguayans, especially in the countryside, gained no benefit from the economic boom and disputes over land and distribution have been frequent. One such confrontation in June 2012 led to 17 deaths and both houses of Congress castigated President Lugo for his handling of the tragedy. Lugo was impeached and forced from office. Vice-president Federico Franco of the Liberal Party took over and Paraguay was expelled from the Mercosur trade group by its partners Argentina, Brazil and Uruguay for the so-called parliamentary coup.

In April 2013, presidential elections were held which were won by Horacio Cartes of the Colorado Party. On his election the Mercosur leaders offered to welcome Paraguay back to the group. Since the Paraguayan Congress had always objected to Venezuela joining Mercosur, and since the other three members had made Venezuela a member while Paraguay was expelled, the Mercosur offer was declined until the impasse was resolved in December 2013.

Cartes, a multi-millionaire businessman, promised in his inaugural speech in August 2013 to tackle poverty, but almost his first act had to be to take on new powers to deal with an outbreak of attacks by EPP in the north of the country. A Plan Nacional de Desarrollo (PND) was developed for 2014-2030, aimed at improving social development, providing economic growth for all sectors of society and opening Paraguay up to international trade markets. Even though raising living standards in the poorest areas was seen as one of the ways of reducing the EPP's influence, critics claimed that after two years in office Cartes had neither stopped the insurgents' activities, nor cut poverty. (An estimated 22.6% of the population – some 1.5 million people – were living below the poverty line in 2015.) Furthermore, the President began to face internal opposition from members of his own Colorado party in the Senate over these measures and political appointments. Economic growth in 2014 was put at 4.5%, with a slow-down in 2015 to around 4% because of reduced electricity output from the Itaipú and Yacyretá dams and the deteriorating economic outlook in neighbours Brazil and Argentina. The prime movers for growth, however, were construction and the agricultural sector, in particular exports of beef. A downside of the success of the livestock sector has been a rush to convert large areas of the Chaco into land for rearing cattle. Hundreds of thousands of hectares have been deforested, including in protected areas, posing a serious threat to uncontacted Ayoreo indigenous people. While Congress has passed laws to preserve the remaining pockets of Atlantic forest in eastern Paraguay, it has rejected any attempt to stop deforestation of the Chaco.

Government

The República del Paraguay's current Constitution was adopted in 1992. The country has 17 departments, with Asunción, the capital, as a separate entity. Executive power rests with the president, elected for five years. There is a two-chamber Congress (Senate 45 seats, Chamber of Deputies 80).

Culture

People

Since Spanish influence was less than in many other parts of South America, most people are bilingual, speaking both Spanish and Guaraní. Outside Asunción, most people speak Guaraní by preference. There is a Guaraní theatre, it is taught in private schools, and books and periodicals are published in that tongue, which has official status as the second national language.

According to the 2002 census, the indigenous population is about 87,000, less than 2% of the total population. There are 20 distinct ethnic groups with five different languages, among which Guaraní predominates. The 1981 Law of Native Communities in theory guarantees indigenous rights to ownership of their traditional lands and the maintenance of their culture. See www.tierraviva.org.py.

Fact file

Population in 2013 6.8 million
Population growth 1.16%
Infant mortality rate 20.1 per
 1000 live births
Literacy rate 93.9%
GDP per capita US$8400 (2014)

Arts and crafts

Early Paraguayan art was highly influenced by European styles and much of the artistic output was religious in nature. Among the first to arrive and work with the native population were priests and friars, often using skilled indigenous artisans for the construction and decoration of new churches. Religious paintings and church ornamentation are among the best preserved works of art in the Americas, many made by unnamed local artists working with the religious communities established shortly after the conquest. Arrivals from Europe also brought renaissance, baroque and rococo influences. The colonial period was characterized by a blending of indigenous and European traditions.

The art of the Jesuit missions of Paraguay is characterized first and foremost by its hybrid character. It is European baroque in terms of its overt style (much of it ornate, with gilding, flowing edges and other period mannerisms) and subject matter, usually a litany of saints, Christ and the Virgin Mary. But it also is infused with a strong streak of native imagery (eg the use of mythical creatures, local flora, and abstract figures as embellishments) and sentiment, namely, a strong inclination towards what might be called the mystical. What is most remarkable about this artistic amalgam forged in Paraguay's mission fields is not so much the result, but the fact that it ever happened. Had the Jesuit missionaries been less willing to adapt to and work with the artistic and cultural practices of the Guaraní, and/or had the Guaraní been less willing to adapt to and incorporate European motifs into their artistic output, the result would have been very different. Most likely, it would have been what was so often the case elsewhere in Latin America when the two cultures met: the imposition of one society's views upon the cultural framework of the other.

Instead, the Jesuits and the Guaraní formed a partnership, one that was, all things considered, fairly balanced and centuries ahead of its time (as illustrated in the Martin Scorsese film *The Mission*). The missionaries allowed the natives a free hand in the art that was produced, while the inhabitants of the *reducciones* were eager to accommodate European preferences and represent them through their own eyes. The Guaraní and other peoples were indefatigable when it came to artistic production. They were endlessly talented in creating whatever was needed, be it a small wooden carving or an entire church complex, a single drum or an entire orchestra with a complete score in Latin. Well ahead of their contemporaries in acculturation, the Jesuit (and to a lesser extent, Franciscan) missionaries considered art an international language that served a number of purposes. While language could create formidable boundaries, art could communicate across disparate cultures, allowing all groups in the mission environment an opportunity to find a common form of expression. In colonial Paraguay, art was a form of preaching that visually expressed and impressed the tenets of Christianity, an invaluable aid in conveying them to an illiterate populace. Indigenous groups, on the other hand, used art to express their ethnic identities by blending native styles and iconographies with Christian subjects.

For all of South America, with the notable exceptions of Bolivia and Paraguay, whose indigenous populations had developed a unique artistic synthesis with Jesuit missionaries in the region, it was mostly the newly arrived Europeans who were mixing the styles and influences, while many of the native communities did their utmost to keep their traditions intact. After independence, a much greater exchange began, with Europeans (especially from England and Spain) coming over to Paraguay to teach, while in turn many wealthy Paraguayans visited Europe, returning with new skills, techniques and knowledge. As with literary output, art and artistic expression have been strongly influenced by the politics of the region. Independence movements, in particular, fuelled a continent-wide reassessment of what it meant to be 'American' and there was a widespread search for identity away from the colonial powers that played a key part in all forms of culture of the time. Despite this, many artists, art historians and scholars continued to be educated abroad, more often than not in Europe, thus continuing European influence over Paraguayan art in the centuries that have followed independence.

Popular handicrafts in Paraguay

Paraguay has an abundance of different traditional handicrafts that have developed over time. Its distinctive crafts often show a mixture of indigenous and European influences and reflect the largely agrarian and rural nature of its society.

Textiles and weaving These have been of great importance throughout Paraguay from an economic, as well as a social and spiritual-religious perspective. The materials used in producing textiles have included fibres from trees, plants and shrubs, hemp, hides, bird feathers, human hair, horsehair and cotton, as well as the wool from llamas, alpacas, vicuñas and sheep. Traditional weaving goes back thousands of years. The skills were to be exploited in colonial times, in large-scale *mitas*, textile workshops, and the Spaniards were soon exporting cloth to Europe. For the native population, however, textiles, apart from their utilitarian functions, were also used for rituals and ceremonies. These items often had intricate designs and patterns. It is still the case that in the more remote areas of the country, different communities wear different traditional outfits – at least for festivals and other cultural events – some introduced by the conquistadors, some of more ancient origin.

Jewellery and metalwork These are also traditions with several thousand years of history. Copper, gold and platinum were all mined before the arrival of the Spaniards and although many of the objects of the early civilizations were functional in nature, intricately ornate jewellery and ceremonial knives have been found at archaeological sites. Precious and semi-precious stones were often used in ceremonial costumes and at burials, since metal objects on their own were not considered of worth. Ironwork was introduced to South America after the conquest and many skilled Spaniards and Italians, in particular, arrived to develop new metalworking techniques. Silverwork came to be strongly associated with the gaucho culture across Uruguay, parts of northern Argentina, southern Brazil and Paraguay. Although this culture is no longer a dominant one in Paraguay, many riding accessories are still forged from silver, along with the obligatory mate gourd with silver inlays.

Basketry and fibre crafts Basketry, hat-making and bag-making are very common and often provide a means of employment and income for indigenous populations in the Paraguayan Chaco. Woven bags are household items in many parts of the country and shopping bags are as likely to be made from natural materials as they are from plastic. Hats, fans, mats and boxes are also common items found in many Paraguayan homes. Reeds, palm fibre, bamboo, horsehair, maguey and cane are just some of the many different materials used.

Pottery Pottery is perhaps the oldest craft in South America. Pre-Columbian pottery, although not commonly found in Paraguay, often carried religious or magical symbolism and although many objects were functional in nature, others carried highly spiritual significance. The skilled artisans of Paraguay mix ceramic tiles with woodcarving.

Other popular crafts The art of making wind musical instruments and drums goes back to pre-Columbian times, while the Spanish introduced stringed instruments to the continent. Materials used include ceramic, wood and gourds, as well as bamboo, particularly for the wind instruments. However, Paraguay is best known for its matchless acoustic guitars and of course, the Paraguayan harp. Guaraní and Mestizo instrument makers were entrepreneurs in Paraguay, and the local music came to reflect Guaraní folklore and legends and appreciation of their environment in songs largely about birds, women and Guaraní lore. The Paraguayan harp became the national instrument of the country, its historical roots associated with liberation from the missionary systems of the more repressive neighbouring countries. For many, it is the national symbol of Paraguay.

Between the 1930s and late 1950s, beautifully carved Paraguayan harps had influence across the world and many famous Paraguayan performers toured Europe and South America, usually with both the Paraguayan harp and an acoustic guitar (ideally suited to accompany the harp) in tow. Paraguayan harp is played solo or in duet with another harp, a guitar or a violin. In Paraguay itself, it often accompanies singing in Guaraní or Spanish or a mixture of the two, and is played mostly by men. Guaraní tradition prohibited women from playing music, for religious reasons, and women did not play the Paraguayan harp at all until the late 20th century

Many intricate religious figurines, especially of Saint Francis of Assisi and the Virgin of Caacupé (Paraguay's patron saint), influenced by the Jesuits and a reflexion of the country's religious history, hail from Paraguay. Most of these are wooden or ceramic objects, and are beautifully dyed with resin or painted in bright colours.

Land & environment

Paraguay has a land area of 406,752 sq km. It is a landlocked country, divided into two distinct regions by the Río Paraguay. Eastern Paraguay combines habitats characteristic of three ecoregions: *cerrado* (a mosaic of dry forest and savannah habitats) in the north, humid Atlantic forest in the east, and natural grasslands and marshes in the south. West of the river lies the vast expanse of the Chaco, comprising seasonally flooded palm-savannahs in the southeast, semi-arid thorn scrub-forest to the west, and in the north, the Pantanal, part of the world's largest wetland. The Río Paraná forms part of the eastern and southern boundaries of the country but the rivers are so difficult to navigate that communication with Buenos Aires, 1450 km from Asunción, has been mainly on land.

Eastern Paraguay is the 40% of the country east of the Río Paraguay, a rich land of rolling hills in which the vast majority of the population live. An escarpment runs north from the Río Alto Paraná, west of Encarnación, to the Brazilian border. East of this escarpment the Paraná Plateau extends across neighbouring parts of Argentina and Brazil. The plateau, which is crossed by the Río Paraná, ranges from 300-600 m in height, was originally forest and enjoys relatively high levels of rainfall. West and south of the escarpment and stretching to the Río Paraguay lies a fertile plain with wooded hills, drained by several tributaries of the Río Paraná. Most of the population of Paraguay lives in these hilly lands, stretching southeast from the capital to Encarnación. The area produces timber, cotton, hides and semi-tropical products. Closer to the rivers, much of the plain is flooded once a year; it is wet savanna, treeless, but covered with coarse grasses. The Chaco, about 60% of the country's area, is a flat, infertile plain stretching north along the west bank of the Río Paraguay. The marshy, largely unnavigable Río Pilcomayo, flowing southeast across the Chaco to join the Río Paraguay near Asunción, forms the frontier with Argentina. The landscape is dominated by the alluvial material brought down in the past by rivers from the Andes. As the rainfall diminishes westwards, the land can support little more than scrub and cacti. The arrival of the Mennonites in the 1930s in the Chaco brought some intense production of fruit and other crops.

Practicalities
Paraguay

Getting there

All countries in Latin America (in fact across the world) officially require travellers entering their territory to have an onward or return ticket and may at times ask to see that ticket. Although rarely enforced at airports, this regulation can create problems at border crossings. In lieu of an onward ticket out of the country you are entering, any ticket out of another Latin American country may sometimes suffice, or proof that you have sufficient funds to buy a ticket (a credit card will do).

Air

Flights from Europe

At the time of writing, Paraguay did not have direct flights from Europe, but **Air Europa** was due to start Madrid–Asunción flights in December 2015. Other than that route, flights to Asunción involve at least one stopover in another South American country. In many cases, though, the choice of departure point is limited to Madrid and one or two other cities (Paris or Amsterdam, for instance). Argentina, Brazil and Venezuela have the most options.

Flights from North America

Where there are no direct flights, connections can be made in the USA (Miami, or other gateways), Buenos Aires, Rio de Janeiro or São Paulo. The main US gateways are Miami, Houston, Dallas, Atlanta and New York. On the west coast, Los Angeles has flights to several South American cities. If buying airline tickets routed through the USA, check that US taxes are included in the price. Flights from Canada are mostly via the USA, although there are direct flights from Toronto to Bogotá and Santiago.

Flights from other areas

Likewise, flights from Australia and New Zealand are best through Los Angeles, except for the **Qantas/LAN** route from Sydney and Auckland to Santiago, and Qantas' non-stop route Sydney to Santiago, from where connections can be made. From Japan and from South Africa there are direct flights to Brazil.

Flights from Latin America

Within Latin America there is plenty of choice on local carriers and some connections on US or European airlines.

Departure tax

US$41, payable on departure in US$ or guaraníes (cheaper).

Getting around

Air

There are 11 airports in Paraguay, seven of which have commercial facilities. Of these, only Asunción's Silvio Petrossi and Ciudad del Este's Guaraní airports have international flights (Mariscal Estigarribia's Luis Argaña and Pedro Juan Caballero's Augusto Fuster airports are designated as international but do not currently have any services), meaning if you arrive or leave by air it will be via one of these two airports. There are scheduled services between these two airports (generally five per day) but all other domestic flights are private.

Departure tax Domestic fares are subject to US$6 tax, payable in dollars or guaraníes. For international departure tax, see page 131.

Bus

Along most main roads, buses will stop at almost any junction to collect or drop off passengers, so all timetables are approximate.

Train

Most of the 441-km rail network closed in early 2001, with the last stretch sealed off in 2012. Neither freight trains to Encarnación, nor the tourist steam train service (*Tren del Lago*) from Asunción's Botánico station, to Sapucai via Areguá is now run. A large number of components of the historic railway system were dismantled and sold for scrap. Plans to recommence tourist trains have come and gone, but in 2015 **Ferrocarriles del Paraguay (FEPASA)** was seeking investment for an electric light railway would run from Asunción to Ypacaraí via Luque by 2017, with a continuation eventually to Encarnación.

Maps

A general map of the country can be purchased at most bookstores in Asunción and at bus terminals. The **Touring y Automóvil Club Paraguayo** (TACPy, www. tacpy.com.py), publishes an annual guide (latest edition 2010) in Spanish and English, with maps, US$27, but more detailed maps are available from **Servicio Geográfico Militar** ① *Av Artigas 920, T021-204959*; take your passport.

ON THE ROAD
Driving in Paraguay

Road Around 10% of roads are paved. Roads serving the main centres are in good condition and are continually being upgraded. A highway links Asunción with Iguazú Falls (six hours). Potholes are a hazard, especially in Asunción. Unsurfaced roads may not be passable in bad weather, especially November-April. There are regular police checks; it's advisable to lock doors.

Safety Beware of stray cattle on the road at night. Driving at night is not advisable.

Documents Neither a *carnet de passages* nor *libreta de pasos por aduana* is required for a car or motorcycle, but the carnet may make entry easier. Temporary admission for a private vehicle is usually 30 days.

Organizations Touring y Automóvil Club Paraguayo (TACP), 25 de Mayo y Brasíl, p 2, Asunción, T021-210550, www.tacpy.com.py, produces a road map and provides information about weather and roads. Information also from the office of the traffic police in Asunción, T021-493390 (DIRECCIONPMT on Facebook).

Car hire Weekly and free-kilometre rates available. Rates from US$42 per day to US$70 for 4WD.

Fuel Unleaded only (some has sugar-cane alcohol added). Most vehicles are diesel-powered. 85 octane US$0.76 per litre; special US$0.93 per litre; super US$1.07 per litre; diesel US$0.83 per litre. Motor fuel and oil are sold by the litre. There are few service stations in the Chaco.

Essentials A-Z

Accident and emergency

Ambulance and police emergency T911.

Disabled travellers

In most of South America, facilities for the disabled are severely lacking. For those in wheelchairs, ramps and toilet access are limited to some of the more upmarket, or most recently built hotels. Pavements are often in a poor state of repair or crowded with street vendors. Most archaeological sites have little or no wheelchair access. Visually or hearing-impaired travellers are also poorly catered for, but there are experienced guides in some places who can provide individual attention. There are also travel companies outside South America who specialize in holidays which are tailor-made for the individual's level of disability. While disabled South Americans have to rely on others to get around, foreigners will find that people are generally very helpful. The **Global Access – Disabled Travel Network** website, www.globalaccessnews.com/index.htm, is useful. Another informative site, with lots of advice on how to travel with specific disabilities, plus listings and links belongs to the **Society for Accessible Travel and Hospitality**, www.sath.org.

Electricity

220 volts AC, 50Hz cycles, but power surges and voltage drops are frequent. European 2 round-pin plugs are used. Visitors from North America should bring an adaptor, as few hotels outside Asunción offer 110-volt service.

Embassies and consulates

For Paraguayan embassies and consulates abroad and for all foreign embassies and consulates in Paraguay, see http://embassy.goabroad.com.

Health

See your GP or travel clinic at least 6 weeks before departure for general advice on travel risks and vaccinations. Try phoning a specialist travel clinic if your own doctor is unfamiliar with health in the region. Make sure you have sufficient medical travel insurance, get a dental check, know your own blood group and, if you suffer a long-term condition such as diabetes or epilepsy, obtain a **Medic Alert** bracelet (www.medicalert.org.uk).

Vaccinations and anti-malarials

Confirm that your primary courses and boosters are up to date. It is advisable to vaccinate against polio, tetanus, typhoid, hepatitis A and, for more remote areas, rabies. Yellow fever vaccination is obligatory for most areas. Cholera, diphtheria and hepatitis B vaccinations are sometimes advised. Specialist advice should be taken on the best antimalarials to take before you leave.

Health risks

The major risks posed in the region are those caused by insect disease carriers such as mosquitoes and sandflies. The key parasitic and viral diseases are malaria, South American trypanosomiasis (Chagas' disease) and dengue fever. Be aware that you are always at risk from these diseases. **Malaria** is a danger throughout the lowland tropics and coastal regions. **Dengue fever**, which is widespread, is particularly hard to protect against as the mosquitoes can bite throughout the day as well as night (unlike those that carry malaria). In 2015 cases of the **chikungunya virus**, transmitted by the same mosquito that carries dengue, had been confirmed. Try to wear clothes that cover arms and legs and also use effective mosquito repellent. Mosquito nets dipped in permethrin provide a good physical and chemical barrier at night. **Chagas' disease** is spread by faeces of the triatomine, or assassin bugs, whereas sandflies spread a disease of the skin called **leishmaniasis**.

Some form of **diarrhoea** or intestinal upset is almost inevitable, the standard advice is always to wash your hands before eating and to be careful with drinking water and ice; if you have any doubts about the water then boil it or filter and treat it. In a restaurant buy bottled water or ask where the water has come from. Food can also pose a problem, be wary of salads if you don't know whether they have been washed or not.

There is a constant threat of **tuberculosis** (TB) and although the BCG vaccine is available, it is still not guaranteed protection. It is best to avoid unpasteurized dairy products and try not to let people cough and splutter all over you.

Another risk, especially to campers and people with small children, is that of the **hanta virus**, which is carried by some forest and riverine rodents. Symptoms are a flu-like illness, which can lead to complications. Try as far as possible to avoid rodent-infested areas, especially close contact with rodent droppings.

If you get sick

Make sure you have adequate insurance (see below). Contact your embassy or consulate for a list of doctors and dentists who speak your language, or at least some English. Your hotel may also be able to recommend good local medical services. The following are in Asunción.

Chemists

Farmacia y Perfumería Catedral, *Av España esq Santa Ana, Villa Mora, Asunción, T021-600723, www. farmaciacatedral.com.py.* Incredible range, old-fashioned 'wood and marble' chemist, like going back 60 years, courteous staff with different stages to the buying process. 40 branches throughout Asunción.

Private hospitals

Centro Médico Bautista, *Av Argentina y Cervera, Asunción, T021-688 9000, www. cmb.org.py.*
Sanatorio San Roque, *Eligio Ayala y Pa'í Pérez, Asunción, T021-248 9000, www. sanroque.com.py,* 24 hrs.

Public hospital

Centro de Emergencias Médicas, *Av Gral Santos y Teodoro S Mongelos, Asunción, T021-204800, www.cem.gov.py.*

Further information
Centres for Disease Control and Prevention (USA), www.cdc.gov.

www.nhs.uk/nhsengland/
healthcareabroad
Fit for Travel (UK), www.fitfortravel.scot.
nhs.uk, a site from Scotland providing
a quick A-Z of vaccine and travel health
advice requirements for each country.
**National Travel Health Network and
Centre (NaTHNaC)**, www.nathnac.org.
**Institute for Tropical Medicine,
Antwerp**, www.itg.be.
World Health Organisation,
www.who.int.

Insurance

We strongly recommend that you invest
in a good insurance policy that covers
you for theft or loss of possessions
and money, the cost of medical and
dental treatment, cancellation of
flights, delays in travel arrangements,
accidents, missed departures, lost
baggage and lost passport. Be sure
to check on inclusion of 'dangerous
activities' if you plan on doing any.
These generally include climbing, diving,
skiing, horse riding, parachuting, even
trekking. You should always read the
small print carefully. Not all policies
cover ambulance, helicopter rescue or
emergency flights home.

There are a variety of policies to
choose from, so it's best to shop around.
Your travel agent can advise on the best
deals available. Reputable student travel
organizations often offer good-value
policies. Travellers from North America
can try the **International Student
Insurance Service (ISIS)**, which is
available through **STA**, T800-7814040,
www.statravel.com. Companies worth
trying in Britain include **Direct Line
Insurance**, T0845-246 8704, www.
directline.com, and the **Flexicover
Group**, T0800-093 9495, www.flexicover.

net. Some companies will not cover
those over 65. The best policies for older
travellers are through **Age UK**, T0845-
600 3348, www.ageuk.org.uk.

Internet

Internet speed is relatively slow, but
improving, and there are plans to install
free Wi-Fi points in many cities by 2015
and to improve coverage in rural areas
by 2017.

Language

See page 143 for basic Spanish words
and phrases. The official language of the
majority of South American countries is
Spanish. Guaraní is the second official
language. Most people are bilingual
and, outside Asunción, speak Guaraní.
Many people speak a mixture of the 2
languages known as *jopara*. English is
often spoken by wealthy and well-
educated citizens, but otherwise the use
of English is generally restricted to those
working in the tourism industry. The
basic Spanish of Hispanic America is that
of southwestern Spain, with soft 'c's and
'z's' pronounced as 's', and not as 'th' as
in the other parts of Spain.

Without some knowledge of Spanish
you will become very frustrated and feel
helpless in many situations. English, or
any other language, is absolutely useless
off the beaten track. Some initial study,
to get you up to a basic vocabulary of
500 words or so, and a pocket dictionary
and phrase-book, are most strongly
recommended: your pleasure will be
doubled if you can talk to the locals.

US$1 = ₲5220, UK£1= ₲8166,
€1= ₲5799 (Aug 2015)

Currency

The guaraní (plural guaraníes) is the unit of currency, symbolized by ₲. There are bank notes for 2000, 5000, 10,000, 20,000, 50,000 and 100,000 guaraníes and coins for 50, 100, 500 and 1000 guaraníes. Coins of 50 and 100 guaraníes are essentially worthless at current rates. Get rid of all your guaraníes before leaving Paraguay; there is no market for them elsewhere.

ATMs, credit and currency cards

Asunción is a good place for obtaining US$ cash on MasterCard or Visa especially if heading for Brazil. ATMs for Visa and MasterCard are common in Asunción and offer good rates of exchange. They accept credit and debit cards and give dollars and guaraníes. Many banks in Asunción (eg **HSBC, Citibank, ABN AMRO, Interbanco**) give US$ cash, but charge up to 5.5% commission. Rates for most other foreign currencies are reasonable.

Casas de cambio

Many *casas de cambio* on Palma, Estrella and nearby streets in the capital (Mon-Fri 0730-1200, 1500-1830, Sat 0730-1200). All rates are better than at frontiers. They change dollars, euros, Brazilian reais, Argentine pesos and a few will accept sterling notes or Bolivianos. *Casas de cambio* and banks may want to see customers' records of purchase before accepting TCs. There are many *casas de cambio* in Asunción on Palma, Estrella and nearby streets (Mon-Fri 0730-1200, 1500-1830, Sat 0730-1200); they change dollars, euros, Brazilian reais, Argentine pesos and a few will accept sterling notes or Bolivianos; some change only dollar-denominated TCs. Visa and MasterCard cash advances are possible in Asunción, Ciudad del Este and Encarnación, but only for credit (not debit) cards.

Street dealers operate from early morning until late at night, even on public holidays, but double-check that they are giving you the right exchange (have your own calculator handy) and the right amount of cash. If changing into US$, do not accept very dirty, taped or torn bills; they are not valid in Paraguay.

Cost of travelling

Allow US$50-60 per person per day to cover main expenses, unless staying in the cheapest hotels and not moving around much. Average cost of internet in towns is US$0.75-1.25 per hr.

Banks Mon-Fri 0845-1500.
Government offices 0700-1130 in summer, 0730-1200 in winter, open Sat.
Museums Usually Mon-Fri 0800-1200 and 1330-1700. As a rule, Paraguay does not follow the regional norm of closing its museums on Mon.
Shops, offices and businesses Open around 0700; some may close 1200-1500 for lunch and siesta.

The historic post office at Alberdi, between Benjamín Constant y El Paraguayo Independiente, in Ascunción does not have postal services. The main office is at 25 de Mayo 340 y Yegros, T021-498112, Mon-Fri 0700-2000, Sat 0700-1200. **Poste Restante** (ask at the Casillas section) charges about US$0.50 per item, but you may have to insist they double-check if you are expecting letters. Packages under 2 kg should be handed in at the small packages window, up to 20 kg at the 'Encomiendas' office. A faster and more reliable way to send parcels is by EMS, the post office courier service from the same office. Customs inspection of open parcel required. Register all important mail. There are sub-offices at Shopping del Sol, Mall Excelsior and in certain suburbs, but mail takes longer to arrive from these offices.

Public holidays

1 Jan New Year
1-3 Feb San Blas, patron of Paraguay, but as of 2014 re-named Day of Paraguayan Democracy to commemorate the overthrow of the dictator Alfredo Stroessner in 1989.
1 Mar National Heroes' Day, on the anniversary of the death of former president Francisco Solano López.
Easter Wed of Holy Week; Maundy Thu; Good Friday.
1 May Labour Day.
14 May Independence.
12 Jun Paz del Chaco.
24 Jun San Juan.
15 Aug Founding of Asunción.
16 Aug Children's Day, in honour of the boys who died at the Battle of Acosta Ñu, see page 22.
29 Sep Victory of Boquerón, decisive battle in the Chaco War.
8 Dec Virgen de Caacupé/Inmaculada Concepción.
25 Dec Christmas Day.

Safety

Paraguay is generally safe and visitors are treated courteously. At election times there may be demonstrations in the capital, but the country as a whole is calm. Travellers heading to Pedro Juan Caballero should be aware that drug smuggling is an ongoing problem. Likewise, contraband goods are everywhere in Ciudad del Este and should be avoided. Beware police seeking bribes, especially at Asunción bus station and at border crossings.

Tax

Airport tax See page 131 for international departures and page 132 for domestic ones.
VAT/IVA 10% (5% for some purchases).

Telephone *Country code +595*

Ringing: equal long tones with long pauses. **Engaged**: equal short tones with equal pauses. **Directory enquiries and information**: T112. To make local calls, just the 5-, 6- or 7-digit subscriber number is used. (At present, only a few cities, such as Asunción, Ciudad del Este and Villarrica have 7-digit numbers as well as 6-digit ones.) To make calls between different towns, an access code ('0') followed by the 2- or 3- (in rare cases, 4-) digit city code are required, then the 6-or 7-digit subscriber number. The access code is not part of the city code.

There are 4 mobile carriers that operate in Paraguay, and each has its own 3-digit prefix: **Claro** (991-3 and 995); **Personal** (971-3 and 975-6); **Tigo** (the largest provider, with prefixes 981-5); and **VOX** (sometimes called **Hola**, 961 and 963). These prefixes take the place of city codes and are followed immediately by the 6-digit subscriber number. There is no access code ('0') needed with mobile numbers within Paraguay. There is very high mobile telephone usage in rural Paraguay, much more so than traditional landline use, which is more expensive. If given 2 numbers to call when outside a major city, try the mobile one first. You can use a prepaid SIM card, with prior registration at one of the official carrier's offices. Because of the relatively underfunded fixed-line telephone and broadband service, most growth has been in the mobile sector.

Time

Standard time GMT -4 hrs begins early Apr. Summer time GMT -3 hrs begins early Oct (dates change yearly).

Tipping

Restaurants, 10%. **Taxis**, 10%. In supermarkets, tip the check-out boys who pack bags; they are not paid.

Tourist information

Secretaría Nacional de Turismo (Senatur), Palma 468 y 14 de Mayo, Asunción, T021-494110/441530, www.senatur.gov.py or www.paraguay.travel.

Useful websites
http://discoveringparaguay.com/home: a blog about living and travelling in Paraguay.
www.cabildoccr.gov.py: the Centro Cultural de la República El Cabildo's (the government's official cultural promotion arm) website (in Spanish).
www.lanic.utexas.edu/la/sa/paraguay: enormous bilingual portal for information on all things Paraguay,

maintained by University of Texas' Latin American Network Information Center.
www.presidencia.gov.py: the government's official website (in Spanish).
www.quickguide.com.py: regularly updated information on events and happenings in Asunción, Ciudad del Este, Encarnación and San Bernardino.
See Asunción, Entertainment (page 33) for online newspapers.

Visas and immigration

A passport valid for 6 months after the intended length of stay is required to enter Paraguay and tourist visas are issued at the point of entry for a stay of up to 90 days. Visas are extendible for an additional 180 days for US$40 for each 90-day period, after which an overstay fine applies. Visitors are registered on arrival by the immigration authorities and proof of onward travel is required (although not always asked for). Citizens of the following countries do not require visas in advance: EU member states, Israel, Japan, Norway, South Africa, Switzerland, countries of South and Central America.

Citizens of the following countries require visas either in advance or upon arrival (*visa en arribo*) only at Silvio Pettirossi International Airport (not available in Ciudad del Este): valid for 90 days only, the costs are as follows: Australia (US$135), Canada (US$150), New Zealand (US$140), Russia (US$160), Taiwan (US$100) and the United States (US$160). Fees are payable in these countries' respective national currencies or guaraníes only; credit cards not accepted. Only citizens of the countries listed above can obtain a visa upon arrival. Citizens of all others countries other than the 2 groups above must apply in advance at a Paraguayan embassy or consulate in person (not by mail) for a fee of US$60-65 for single entry, US$100 multiple entry. Present a valid passport, a passport photo, a covering letter and proof of onward travel and economic solvency.

Always double-check in advance at www.mre.gov.py which nationalities need a visa, how much they cost and which Paraguayan consulates issue them. Make sure you're stamped in and out of Paraguay to avoid future problems. If you do not get an entrance stamp in your passport you can be turned back at the border when leaving the country, or have to pay a fine of US$45 or the equivalent in guaraníes. Paraguay's main immigration office (T021-446066, www.migraciones.gov. py) is located at Eligio Ayala y Caballero in Asunción and is open daily 0700-1300.

Weights and measures

Metric.

Footnotes
Paraguay

Basic Spanish for travellers

Learning Spanish is a useful part of the preparation for a trip to Latin America and no volumes of dictionaries, phrase books or word lists will provide the same enjoyment as being able to communicate directly with the people of the country you are visiting. It is a good idea to make an effort to grasp the basics before you go. As you travel you will pick up more of the language and the more you know, the more you will benefit from your stay.

General pronunciation

Whether you have been taught the 'Castilian' pronunciation (*z* and *c* followed by *i* or *e* are pronounced as the *th* in think) or the 'American' pronunciation (they are pronounced as *s*), you will encounter little difficulty in understanding either. Regional accents and usages vary, but the basic language is essentially the same everywhere.

Vowels

a as in English *cat*
e as in English *best*
i as the *ee* in English *feet*
o as in English *shop*
u as the *oo* in English *food*
ai as the *i* in English *ride*
ei as *ey* in English *they*
oi as *oy* in English *toy*

Consonants

Most consonants can be pronounced more or less as they are in English. The exceptions are:

g before *e* or *i* is the same as *j*
h is always silent (except in *ch* as in *chair*)
j as the *ch* in Scottish *loch*
ll as the *y* in *yellow*
ñ as the *ni* in English *onion*
rr trilled much more than in English
x depending on its location, pronounced *x*, *s*, *sh* or *j*

Spanish words and phrases

Greetings, courtesies

hello *hola*
good morning *buenos días*
good afternoon/evening/night
  buenas tardes/noches
goodbye *adiós/chao*
pleased to meet you *mucho gusto*
see you later *hasta luego*
how are you? *¿cómo está?/¿cómo estás?*
I'm fine, thanks *estoy muy bien, gracias*

I'm called... *me llamo...*
what is your name? *¿cómo se llama?/*
  ¿cómo te llamas?
yes/no *sí/no*
please *por favor*
thank you (very much) *(muchas) gracias*
I speak Spanish *hablo español*
I don't speak Spanish *no hablo español*
do you speak English? *¿habla inglés?*

I don't understand *no entiendo/ no comprendo*
please speak slowly *hable despacio por favor*
I am very sorry *lo siento mucho/disculpe*
what do you want? *¿qué quiere?/ ¿qué quieres?*

I want *quiero*
I don't want it *no lo quiero*
good/bad *bueno/malo*
leave me alone *déjeme en paz/ no me moleste*

Questions and requests

Have you got a room for two people? *¿Tiene una habitación para dos personas?*
How do I get to_? *¿Cómo llego a_?*
How much does it cost? *¿Cuánto cuesta? ¿cuánto es?*
I'd like to make a long-distance phone call *Quisiera hacer una llamada de larga distancia*
Is service included? *¿Está incluido el servicio?*

Is tax included? *¿Están incluidos los impuestos?*
When does the bus leave (arrive)? *¿A qué hora sale (llega) el autobús?*
When? *¿cuándo?*
Where is_? *¿dónde está_?*
Where can I buy tickets? *¿Dónde puedo comprar boletos?*
Where is the nearest petrol station? *¿Dónde está la gasolinera más cercana?*
Why? *¿por qué?*

Basics

bank *el banco*
bathroom/toilet *el baño*
bill *la factura/la cuenta*
cash *el efectivo*
cheap *barato/a*
credit card *la tarjeta de crédito*
exchange house *la casa de cambio*
exchange rate *el tipo de cambio*

expensive *caro/a*
market *el mercado*
note/coin *le billete/la moneda*
police (policeman) *la policía (el policía)*
post office *el correo*
public telephone *el teléfono público*
supermarket *el supermercado*
ticket office *la taquilla*

Getting around

aeroplane *el avión*
airport *el aeropuerto*
arrival/departure *la llegada/salida*
avenue *la avenida*
block *la cuadra*
border *la frontera*
bus station *la terminal de autobuses/ camiones*
bus *el bus/el autobús/el camión*
collective/fixed-route taxi *el colectivo*
corner *la esquina*
customs *la aduana*
first/second class *primera/segunda clase*

left/right *izquierda/derecha*
ticket *el boleto*
empty/full *vacío/lleno*
highway, main road *la carretera*
immigration *la inmigración*
insurance *el seguro*
insured person *el/la asegurado/a*
to insure yourself against *asegurarse contra*
luggage *el equipaje*
motorway, freeway *el autopista/ la carretera*

north, south, east, west *norte, sur, este (oriente), oeste (occidente)*
oil *el aceite*
to park *estacionarse*
passport *el pasaporte*
petrol/gasoline *la gasolina*
puncture *el pinchazo/la ponchadura*

street *la calle*
that way *por allí/por allá*
this way *por aquí/por acá*
tourist card/visa *la tarjeta de turista*
tyre *la llanta*
unleaded *sin plomo*
to walk *caminar/andar*

Accommodation

air conditioning *el aire acondicionado*
all-inclusive *todo incluido*
bathroom, private *el baño privado*
bed, double/single *la cama matrimonial/ sencilla*
blankets *las cobijas/mantas*
to clean *limpiar*
dining room *el comedor*
guesthouse *la casa de huéspedes*
hotel *el hotel*
noisy *ruidoso*
pillows *las almohadas*

power cut *el apagón/corte*
restaurant *el restaurante*
room/bedroom *el cuarto/la habitación*
sheets *las sábanas*
shower *la ducha/regadera*
soap *el jabón*
toilet *el sanitario/excusado*
toilet paper *el papel higiénico*
towels, clean/dirty *las toallas limpias/ sucias*
water, hot/cold *el agua caliente/fría*

Health

aspirin *la aspirina*
blood *la sangre*
chemist *la farmacia*
condoms *los preservativos, los condones*
contact lenses *los lentes de contacto*
contraceptives *los anticonceptivos*
contraceptive pill *la píldora anti-conceptiva*
diarrhoea *la diarrea*

doctor *el médico*
fever/sweat *la fiebre/el sudor*
pain *el dolor*
head *la cabeza*
period/sanitary towels *la regla/las toallas femeninas*
stomach *el estómago*
altitude sickness *el soroche*

Family

family *la familia*
friend *el amigo/la amiga*
brother/sister *el hermano/la hermana*
daughter/son *la hija/el hijo*
father/mother *el padre/la madre*
husband/wife *el esposo (marido)/ la esposa*
boyfriend/girlfriend *el novio/la novia*
married *casado/a*
single/unmarried *soltero/a*

Months, days and time

January *enero*
February *febrero*
March *marzo*
April *abril*
May *mayo*
June *junio*
July *julio*
August *agosto*
September *septiembre*
October *octubre*
November *noviembre*
December *diciembre*

Monday *lunes*
Tuesday *martes*
Wednesday *miércoles*

Thursday *jueves*
Friday *viernes*
Saturday *sábado*
Sunday *domingo*

at one o'clock *a la una*
at half past two *a las dos y media*
at a quarter to three *a cuarto para las tres/a las tres menos quince*
it's one o'clock *es la una*
it's seven o'clock *son las siete*
it's six twenty *son las seis y veinte*
it's five to nine *son las nueve menos cinco*
in ten minutes *en diez minutos*
five hours *cinco horas*
does it take long? *¿tarda mucho?*

Numbers

one *uno/una*
two *dos*
three *tres*
four *cuatro*
five *cinco*
six *seis*
seven *siete*
eight *ocho*
nine *nueve*
ten *diez*
eleven *once*
twelve *doce*
thirteen *trece*
fourteen *catorce*
fifteen *quince*

sixteen *dieciséis*
seventeen *diecisiete*
eighteen *dieciocho*
nineteen *diecinueve*
twenty *veinte*
twenty-one *veintiuno*
thirty *treinta*
forty *cuarenta*
fifty *cincuenta*
sixty *sesenta*
seventy *setenta*
eighty *ochenta*
ninety *noventa*
hundred *cien/ciento*
thousand *mil*

Food

avocado *la palta*
baked *al horno*
bakery *la panadería*
banana *la banana*
beans *los frijoles/las habichuelas*
beef *la carne de res*
beef steak *el lomo*
boiled rice *el arroz blanco*
bread *el pan*

breakfast *el desayuno*
butter *la manteca*
cake *la torta*
chewing gum *el chicle*
chicken *el pollo*
chilli or green pepper *el ají chile/ pimiento*
clear soup, stock *el caldo*
cooked *cocido*

dining room *el comedor*
egg *el huevo*
fish *el pescado*
fork *el tenedor*
fried *frito*
garlic *el ajo*
goat *el chivo*
grapefruit *la toronja/el pomelo*
grill *la parrilla*
grilled/griddled *a la plancha*
guava *la guayaba*
ham *el jamón*
hamburger *la hamburguesa*
hot, spicy *picante*
ice cream *el helado*
jam *la mermelada*
knife *el cuchillo*
lemon *el limón*
lobster *la langosta*
lunch *el almuerzo/la comida*
meal *la comida*
meat *la carne*
minced meat *la carne picada*
onion *la cebolla*
orange *la naranja*
pepper *el pimiento*

pasty, turnover *la empanada/el pastelito*
pork *el cerdo*
potato *la papa*
prawns *los camarones*
raw *crudo*
restaurant *el restaurante*
salad *la ensalada*
salt *la sal*
sandwich *el bocadillo*
sauce *la salsa*
sausage *la longaniza/el chorizo*
scrambled eggs *los huevos revueltos*
seafood *los mariscos*
soup *la sopa*
spoon *la cuchara*
squash *la calabaza*
squid *los calamares*
supper *la cena*
sweet *dulce*
to eat *comer*
toasted *tostado*
turkey *el pavo*
vegetables *los legumbres/vegetales*
without meat *sin carne*
yam *el camote*

Drink
beer *la cerveza*
boiled *hervido/a*
bottled *en botella*
camomile tea *la manzanilla*
canned *en lata*
coffee *el café*
coffee, white *el café con leche*
cold *frío*
cup *la taza*
drink *la bebida*
drunk *borracho/a*
firewater *el aguardiente*
fruit milkshake *el batido/licuado*
glass *el vaso*
hot *caliente*
ice/without ice *el hielo/sin hielo*
juice *el jugo*

lemonade *la limonada*
milk *la leche*
mint *la menta*
rum *el ron*
soft drink *el refresco*
sugar *el azúcar*
tea *el té*
to drink *beber/tomar*
water *el agua*
water, carbonated *el agua mineral con gas*
water, still mineral *el agua mineral sin gas*
wine, red *el vino tinto*
wine, white *el vino blanco*

Key verbs

to go	ir	to be	ser / estar
I go	voy	I am	soy / estoy
you go (familiar)	vas	you are	eres / estás
he, she, it goes, you (formal) go	va	he, she, it is, you (formal) are	es / está
we go	vamos	we are	somos / estamos
they, you (plural) go	van	they, you (plural) are	son / están

(*ser* is used to denote a permanent state, whereas *estar* is used to denote a positional or temporary state.)

to have (possess)	tener
I have	tengo
you (familiar) have	tienes
he, she, it, you (formal) have	tiene
we have	tenemos
they, you (plural) have	tienen
there is/are	hay
there isn't/aren't	no hay

This section has been assembled on the basis of glossaries compiled by André de Mendonça and David Gilmour of South American Experience, London, and the Latin American Travel Advisor, No 9, March 1996.

Index

Entries in bold refer to maps